The Counsellor's Workbook

Developing a Personal Approach

John McLeod

Open University Press

Open University Press
McGraw-Hill Education
McGraw-Hill House
Shoppenhangers Road
Maidenhead
Berkshire
England
SL6 2QL

email: enquiries@openup.co.uk
world wide web: www.openup.co.uk

and Two Penn Plaza, New York, NY 10121–2289, USA

First published 2004

A catalogue record of this book is available from the British Library

ISBN 0335 21552 1

Library of Congress Cataloging-in-Publication Data
CIP data applied for

Typeset by YHT Ltd
Printed in the UK by Bell & Bain Ltd, Glasgow

Contents

Acknowledgements

This Workbook is the product of many years of trying to learn about counselling, and of teaching on counselling courses. Inevitably, the Workbook includes ideas that I have come across in books, articles, training courses I have attended, and colleagues' handouts and worksheets. If I have failed to provide proper recognition to anyone whose ideas have been used, please let me know, so that your contribution can be appropriately acknowledged in future editions.

I have particularly appreciated the comments I have received from my colleagues in Dundee – Joe Armstrong, Siobhan Canavan, Edith Cormack, Noreen Lillie, Mhairi Macmillan, Peter Roberts, Brian Rodgers, Cyndy Rodgers and Dot Weaks.

The support and encouragement of my wife, Julia, and my daughters Kate, Emma and Hannah has been, as ever, essential for the completion of this book.

John McLeod

This is the first edition of the Workbook. Any feedback or comments regarding how you have used the book with your classes, and your suggestions for improving it next time (the email address for the workbook is: helpline_maidenhead@mcgraw-hill.com) will be gratefully received. One of the potential lines of development for the workbook would be to adapt some of it for on-line delivery over the Internet. If you are interested in such a development, then let us know.

How to use the Workbook

Contemporary psychotherapy proposes a framework of theory within which the practitioner may, to a certain degree, reveal ordinary human qualities. By contrast I would suggest that psychotherapy is the manifestation of creative human qualities in a facilitating setting, in which the task of healing is eased by a critical knowledge of the theories and techniques of twentieth-century practitioners.

(Lomas, 1981: 3)

. . . the actual techniques employed by the therapists are of lesser importance than the unique character and personality of the therapists themselves. Therapists select techniques and theories because of who they are as persons: therapy strategies are manifestations of the therapist's personality. The therapist as a person is the instrument of primary influence in the therapy enterprise. A corollary of this principle is that the more a therapist accepts and values himself, or herself, the more effective he or she will be in helping clients come to know and appreciate themselves.

(McConnaughy, 1987: 304)

. . . in the end, each therapist develops his or her own style, and the 'theoretical orientation' falls into the background. What remains salient is a unique personality combining artistry and skill. In this respect, a fine therapist closely resembles a painter, novelist or composer. As is true in all the arts and sciences, few reach the summit.

(Strupp, 1978: 31)

More and more, as time has gone by, I have thought that the usual way of training is not satisfactory in that it does not give enough weight to the general way a person behaves and thinks and feels toward someone who is distressed, to the experience of being with people and of getting as much help as possible from colleagues and supervisors. There is too much stress placed on working with particular techniques . . . I think therapy is very much a personal affair. It is not wise to try to make clones of people by making them Freudians or whatever. Student therapists have to find their own way of being with people that will help them. One can expose them to all sorts of marvellous [theorists], and it will do them a lot of good, but that is not the business. The business is to do with finding their own way, using their own intuition, learning to be themselves in the presence of someone who is asking for help, who is probably putting all kinds of pressures on them.

(Lomas, 1999: 25).

Introduction

> It is recommended that you read through this introduction before attempting any of the learning activities in later sections of the Workbook.

Welcome to *The Counsellor's Workbook: Developing a Personal Approach*. This Workbook has been designed as a resource to be used in conjunction with a textbook (McLeod, *An Introduction to Counselling* 2003) during a particular period within your development as a counsellor. For most people who become counsellors, or who develop a counselling dimension within roles such as nurse or teacher, there is a period of typically three or four years when they undergo intensive learning and training activities. Even if this training is 'part-time', with the person continuing to fulfil other ongoing work and caring roles, it is usual for the person to become fully immersed in the whole process of becoming a counsellor: reading widely, reflecting on relationships with trainers/tutors and fellow learners, making sense of what emerges from personal therapy or groupwork, and seeing clients under supervision for the first time. *An Introduction to Counselling* is a book that has been written to be used at the onset of that journey: it provides a map of the territory. The workbook has been created as a tool for further personal exploration of the ground mapped by *An Introduction to Counselling*. The exercises and questions in the Workbook reflect the themes discussed in *An Introduction to Counselling*, and are intended as pointers: they suggest where to look, but not what to find.

To be a good counsellor, it is necessary to develop a way of being with people that is genuinely grounded in your own personal experience, values, and cultural context. Over and over again, research studies have found that what makes a difference to clients are the personal qualities of the counsellor, and his or her capacity to form an accepting and facilitative relationship. The Workbook has therefore been organized around a series of reflective learning tasks, which invite you to explore aspects of your own life that are relevant to your capacity to offer an effective counselling relationship to others. The aim is to help you to get *inside* the various ideas and approaches that exist within the domain of counselling.

The Workbook gives you an opportunity to document, in your own way, the learning process you are experiencing at a significant phase of your personal development. What you write may be useful for you in terms of essays or reports you write during a training course. It may open up issues that you might wish to work on with a counsellor or therapist. It will also be able to help you to decide what you want to do next – what further training or work possibilities are right for you.

Learning to offer a counselling relationship

There are three key aspects of learning about counselling. These are:

➡ Self-awareness;

➡ Understanding the counselling process;

➡ Practical experience.

Accurate and sensitive *self-awareness* underpins any type of counselling work. No matter what approach to counselling is being used, the main instrument for delivering help or therapy is the person or the counsellor himself or herself. To be a counsellor involves interacting with the person seeking help in a flexible and responsive way. There is no fixed script that a counsellor can follow: almost everything a counsellor does is improvised in the moment. It is essential, therefore, for a counsellor to be able to use him or herself as a resource: to be sensitive to the possible significance of shifts in internal feeling states, to have a sense of how his or her actions might be perceived by another person, to have strategies for staying fresh and alert. Effective counselling builds on the quality of the relationship between the helper and the person being helped, and being a counsellor frequently stretches and challenges a helper's capacity to relate: to cope with endings, confrontation, the experience of deep caring, the intricacy of unravelling impasses. In recognition of these factors, all counselling incorporates an element of *work on self*, for example participating in experiential groupwork, gaining the experience of being a client, or keeping a personal reflective journal. Throughout the Workbook you will find that you are invited to write about yourself, to reflect on your own experience and hopefully to gain new insights into yourself. It is important to experience this process (not only through the medium of a workbook but also through being a client yourself at some point in your life), because this is the process that anyone receiving counselling goes through.

In addition to self-awareness, it is necessary for counsellors to develop a *framework for understanding* what they are doing. There has been much debate about whether it is better for counsellors to stick to one theoretical model (e.g. the person-centred approach of Carl Rogers, or a Freudian psychodynamic approach), or whether it is more effective to piece together an integrated personal model from the various theories that are around. It seems that either of these strategies can work, but that what is crucial as a counsellor is to use concepts and ideas that are coherent and make sense to you, and that you can communicate to the people you are trying to help. The importance of developing a robust framework for understanding really stems from the fact that, quite often, people who come for counselling are confused and confusing. They have exhausted their immediate problem-solving resources such as friends and family. They may be in crisis and feel that everything is chaotic and out of control. They may well be afraid of what they feel is happening to them. And they may, one way or another, push all this stuff on to the counsellor: 'here, *you* deal with all this chaos, fear and confusion'. It is at this point that a counsellor needs to feel secure in his or her grasp of reality. The Workbook, as a consequence, includes many tasks that are intended to give you opportunities to piece together and test out your evolving framework for understanding.

The third key element of counselling training or learning, which goes hand in hand with self-awareness and developing a framework for understanding, is that of *practical experience*. There are three types of practical experience that are particularly relevant. The first involves simply sharing your personal experience with others, and hearing about their experiences. The second type of practical experience concerns practising your counselling and helping skills on and with fellow learners. The third form of practical experience involves being in a real counselling role with someone who has come for help with their problems. This Workbook cannot directly enable you to develop your practical experience. It can give you a chance to reflect on some of your personal experience, but if you want to learn to be competent as a counsellor, or as a user of counselling skills and approaches, then you need to find a situation where you can spend many hours acquiring practical experience. When learning the practice of counselling, it is absolutely essential to be a member of a small peer learning group which meets often enough for a climate of trust and honesty to be created, and in which you can be supported as well as challenged, and can learn to give and receive feedback. Being able to draw upon the knowledge and expertise of a tutor or trainer is important too, to provide guidelines and standards and to model good practice. Many of the learning tasks in the workbook lend themselves to exploration in a small group setting. The depth and sustainability of the learning that you can achieve through using the Workbook will be multiplied many times if you are able to reflect on and explore at least some of the learning tasks in the context of an on-going group.

Using the Workbook

There are more than 80 learning tasks and activities in this Workbook. There is no need to feel that you have to try them all. Some of the tasks may introduce areas of self-reflection, contemplation and dialogue with others that may expand to fill many hours of your time. Other tasks may seem uninteresting, trivial, or evoke a response of 'not yet'. Yet other tasks may stimulate you to read and think around the topic, in advance of tackling the learning activities. It is important to trust your own gut feeling, regarding the best direction for your learning at any one time. This is also, possibly, one of the primary rules of counselling: the client's *readiness* to explore any particular issue is a factor that is taken into account by all the main approaches to counselling (although in different ways). The Workbook has been written as a resource that can be useful for counsellors with different interests and needs, so it is inevitable that there will be some activities that are more relevant for you, while others are less relevant.

The structure of the Workbook is designed to have a beginning and an end. The activities in Section 1 are intended to allow you to explore and honour your own experience and knowledge as a person who can engage constructively and helpfully with others who need to talk about their problems. It is essential that you complete at least four or five of the activities in this section *before* you attempt to begin working with any of the other sections, or before you even look at the exercises in these later sections. There are several activities in later sections, for example, that invite you to reflect theoretically on aspects of your personal story, that you have written in response to the tasks in Section 1. It is best to have already completed as many of your 'personal stories' as possible in an intuitive, expressive, open and spontaneous manner, rather than writing them with half a mind to how they might be interpreted.

The activities in the final section, on integration and expressing your professional identity, are intended to be completed during the latter stages of your use of the Workbook. These are activities that invite you to bring together and review themes and ideas from earlier sections.

The activities in the middle sections – theory, practice and cases – can be taken in any order. Although the Workbook is linked throughout to *An Introduction to Counselling*, it does not follow the textbook page by page or even chapter by chapter. Instead, the Workbook tries to give you an opportunity to think about themes and issues that weave through all of the chapters.

Some practical suggestions

The Workbook is designed as a series of learning tasks, each of which will generate written material. It is recommended that you write or paste what you write into a portfolio or journal, which could be in the form of a paper notebook, ringbinder or files in a folder on your PC. If you are keeping this work in a notebook or binder, it may be useful to include a photocopy of the exercise, so that when you look again in the future at what you have written, you can see the instructions or guidelines to which it was a response.

Many counselling courses require students or trainees to keep personal learning diaries or journals, because it has been found that this is an excellent way of helping people to explore personal experience, reflect on experience, and integrate theory and practice. A learning journal also makes it possible to keep track of personal change and development, and to keep hold of new insights (by writing them down) rather than losing them through forgetting. There is also a lot of evidence that writing can in itself be therapeutic (at some point in the future you may want to suggest to some of your counselling clients that they might want to keep journals). Section 1 of the Workbook offers some guidelines for writing a personal journal. If you are using the Workbook in conjunction with a personal journal, it is useful to give a date and title to each entry, and to make sure that what you write is kept in a safe place (if you are worried about someone else reading your journal, chances are that you will be less free in what you write).

The Workbook deliberately does *not* specify how long each task might take, or how much written material it might generate.

There are no right or wrong answers – what is important is what *you* learn.

Working alone and with others

All of the tasks included in the Workbook are primarily designed to promote individual learning, through personal reflection and writing. This emphasis on person or individual learning is a requirement in any counselling learning programme, and reflects the centrality of self-awareness in counselling. The majority of the activities in the Workbook involve periods of sustained reflection on personally significant topics. There is a great deal that can be learned from this. However, working with other people on these tasks introduces important additional opportunities for learning:

➡ The experience of what it is like to share your feelings and thoughts, and your 'story', with others – for example, how risky does this seem to be, are there things you could say but hold back on?

➡ The response of other people to what you have said – do they appear to be interested, involved, shocked, surprised ...? When others ask questions about what you have offered them, do these trigger new ways of looking at the issue?

➡ Observing and listening to your colleagues sharing their responses to the learning activities – in what ways might this broaden your appreciation of the range of possible perspectives that there might be on an issue?

It can be very helpful, therefore, to have a learning partner or partners, or to be a part of a group, with whom the issues raised by this Workbook can be shared and explored. Such learning alliances may be facilitated by a trainer or tutor (for example, as part of a training course) or may be organized on a peer group basis. In either case, there are ground rules which should be discussed, understood and adhered to. The existence of *confidentiality* is a necessary element: it can be destructive and damaging if personal information that is shared in the context of this type of learning is passed on to others without permission (even if for the best of intentions). The existence of *respect* is also necessary – people learn best at their own pace, and when the conditions are right for them.

Taking responsibility and taking care of yourself

Some of the learning tasks in the Workbook invite you to explore intimate and sensitive parts of your own life. Some of the tasks ask you to write about things that maybe you have never told anyone else, or are emotionally painful.

When using the Workbook, remember that:

➡ You are responsible for your own learning. If a task does not appeal to you, or seems threatening, then don't do it. It is *your* choice;

➡ You don't have to show anyone else what you have written unless you decide to. No-one has the right to see what you have written. It's up to you to share what you are comfortable sharing;

➡ Keep what you write in a safe place;

➡ If there is anything in the Workbook that disturbs you, then it may be helpful to talk it over in confidence with a friend or colleague, a tutor (if you are enrolled on a counselling course), or with a counsellor or spiritual advisor. If you find yourself coming back to a Workbook topic, in your own mind, days after writing about it, then this may be a signal that it has raised a significant issue which may repay discussion with another person.

Your experience of using this Workbook may mirror the experience of being a client in counselling. There may be times when you avoid the Workbook or 'forget' about it. There may be other times when you tackle learning tasks with great energy.

Building a portfolio of experiences and reflections

The Workbook is intended to help you to work towards developing competence as a counsellor, by accumulating a portfolio of notes, stories, and ideas which you can use to inform your thinking about counselling and your confidence in what you bring to the counselling relationship. This portfolio may supplement a learning journal or diary that you keep, or it may be quite separate.

In all likelihood, your assumptions about counselling are implicit rather than explicit. In other words, you may have a 'gut feeling' that some approaches and techniques are better than others (at least for you, or in your work context), but it may be hard to put into words exactly where you stand, and why. The learning tasks in the Workbook give you opportunities to put these ideas into words.

It is essential, in using the Workbook, that you actually take the time to write down your responses to tasks. The process of writing will help you to articulate or 'sort out' your ideas in a focused way. Recording your reflections in writing also makes it possible to add more, later. It allows you to reflect on what you have written, and to 'de-centre' yourself. Writing also enables you to reflect on how you may have changed, or on the different 'voices' or feeling states that appear in your words.

The portfolio will give you a rich supply of experiences and reflections which will help you to explore and define many different aspects of yourself as a counsellor. By the end of your involvement with the workbook, your portfolio could contain:

➡ Your responses to the learning tasks provided in the Workbook;

➡ Material from exercises that may have been used on courses or workshops you have attended;

➡ Notes or excerpts you have taken from books and articles you have read, which are relevant to the task of mapping out your own personal understanding of counselling;

➡ Copies of web pages that have been of interest to you;

➡ Personal reflections.

The Workbook is envisaged as a way of supporting your learning about counselling, through providing a structured way of exploring, recording and analysing key dimensions of your counselling competence. When you have completed training, or moved from a period of learning into a stage in which practice has the predominant call on your time and energy, the pressure to record so much information will not be so great. Although you may well find that you have got into the habit of writing about yourself, and building your personal portfolio, you will probably also find that it has mutated into a style and format that is uniquely your own (like your counselling style!).

It is not helpful to view the Workbook as a self-contained exercise – it should connect with other facets of your learning and practice. Some suggested ways of using your Workbook and portfolio are:

➡ Identifying what you are good at and what you need to work on. During training you will get lots of opportunities to practice on and with colleagues, or discuss issues. What you write in the Workbook can help you to be clear about what would be best for you to focus on. For example, perhaps you can see entries in your Workbook which show over and over again that you have difficulty with challenging people, or with ending relationships. These are maybe key areas for further work, because they are so critical to being a good counsellor;

➡ Building up a pool of ideas and insights that you can draw on when writing articles, giving talks, or for coursework essays, case studies and other assignments;

➡ Integrating what you have learned in personal therapy, experiential groups, and supervision. During training, people often spend a lot of time and effort on their personal therapy or supervision, but find it difficult to link up this learning with their theoretical framework, or their practice;

➡ Helping you to be clear about the issues you might want to explore in personal therapy or supervision;

➡ Being clear about who you are and what you do. Developing a professional identity. When you are interviewed for a job, or if you work in a setting where you need to give clients a leaflet describing your approach, you need to sum up your style and qualities as a counsellor in a few words. Some of the Workbook tasks may help you to clarify your career direction;

➡ As a source of support. Becoming a counsellor can be a stressful or even harrowing business. For example, clients or fellow trainees may give you feedback that is hard to take on board. A learning journal or portfolio is a place where you can begin to look at what they have said, and how you feel, and make some sense of it;

➡ Some learning tasks help you to build up information about local resources that you can use in your role as a counsellor, for example various agencies and facilities that you might suggest that your clients make use of, or details of self-help books, articles and leaflets that clients might find helpful.

These are just some of the more obvious ways of using the Workbook during your period of learning about counselling. What is important is not to see the process of using this Workbook as a chore or empty ritual, but to keep in mind the advantages of gradually building up a portfolio of your knowledge, practice and achievements.

The basic assumptions informing the design of this Workbook

The exercises and guidelines provided in the Workbook reflect a set of assumptions about what counselling is about, and what is involved in becoming a good counsellor. The assumptions about the nature of counselling, which have also informed the writing on the accompanying textbook, *An Introduction to Counselling*, can be summarized as:

➡ There is no single approach to counselling that is more effective or valid than any other. There is clinical and research evidence that supports (and is critical of) all of the established therapeutic approaches. In a professional environment in which a plurality of approaches are applied, and where a counsellor may find herself working alongside colleagues representing a wide array of models, it is essential to be familiar with the principal ideas of all of the mainstream approaches;

➡ Effective counselling is largely dependent on the personal qualities of the counsellor, such as his or her capacity to form a connection with the client, the possession of a model of practice that he or she has worked out for him/herself, and a sufficient degree of consistency between his or her therapeutic approach and who he or she is as a person;

➡ At the heart of counselling is the opportunity it provides for the person to tell (and re-tell) their story, to a listener who will be curious, sensitive and accepting. Good counsellors are people who tune into the rich meaningfulness of the stories that other people tell, and are able to draw on an appreciation of the meaningfulness of their own life story;

➡ Counselling is a highly moral activity, and requires a genuine commitment to truth, honesty and a valuing of relationship and conviviality;

A user-centred definition of counselling is offered on pages 14–16 of *An Introduction to Counselling*

➡ Counsel*ling* is an activity that is much wider than the work of counsell*ors*. Most of the time, people who need to talk find themselves a suitable friend, health worker, teacher or clergy.

The main assumption being made within the Workbook about the process of becoming a counsellor, is that learning about counselling is most effective when it builds on personal experience, and recognizes the existing knowledges, skills and personal qualities of the learner. There is a sequence of learning which is reproduced in this Workbook which begins by inviting exploration and documentation of an area of personal experience, then moves into reflection on the potential meaning or significance of that experience, then makes links with theory and research, before finally giving consideration to implications for practice.

Beyond this emphasis on the importance of developing a *personal* approach, is the idea that being a person involves being *in relation* with others, and that – ultimately – building a personal approach can only be done with the help and collaboration of other people. In terms of becoming a counsellor, there are some relationships that appear to be more or less essential:

➡ Being a member of a peer group which offers support and challenge, over an extended period of time, from a basis of equality of status;

➡ Having contact with mentors – more experienced members of the profession –

who can provide inspiration, affirmation and immersion in the discourse of the profession;

⇒ Being in a client-therapist relationship, in the client's chair, and having personal experience of what this situation feels like, and what makes it work better (and worse).

What this means, of course, is that a workbook such as this can only ever be a resource, or a tool. It can never be a substitute for the real business, which is always about working together with others. But it may, hopefully, provide a structure or a meeting place around which this kind of co-operative learning can take place.

Building on life experience: the foundations of a personal approach

The experience of changing your own behaviour

The role of therapy in your life-story

How relevant is spirituality?

How do you cope under pressure?

Do you have a preferred learning style?

What motivates you?

Reflecting on the experience of writing about yourself

Introduction

This section of the Workbook contains a series of tasks that invite you to write about various aspects of your own life. To be a counsellor involves being able to draw upon your own experience, as a means of relating to the people you are trying to help. Your own life-story therefore becomes a resource, within which you can find meaning in response to the issues presented by those who visit you for help.

The writing tasks in this chapter serve two purposes, in relation to developing counselling competence. First, they require you to explore both difficult and hidden, and also joyful, moments in your own life. They are intended to encourage you to look at yourself in terms of certain key questions:

 What are my strengths and gifts, in connection with the task of being a counsellor for another person?

 What are my areas of vulnerability or uncertainty in relation to the activity of counselling?

 What is my own personal understanding, arising from my life experience, of core therapeutic processes such as initiating and maintaining change, sustaining satisfying relationships with others, and taking account of the ways in which my childhood and cultural environment have shaped my behaviour and identity?

By writing openly, honestly and in detail about your life, you can begin to build what narrative therapists call a 'thick description' of your identity as a counsellor: 'thin description allows little space for the complexities and contradictions of life ... . It allows little space for people to articulate their own particular meanings of their actions and the context within which they occurred' (Morgan, 2000: 12). By contrast, a *thick* story is one that is 'richly described', in which the intricacy of one's story, and the way it interlocks with the stories of other people, is expressed. A *thick* story encompasses multiple possibilities, in terms of what it says about the person's capacity to act and feel.

Furthermore, several exercises in later sections of the Workbook make reference to the writing tasks in this chapter. You will be invited to reflect on what you have written here from a range of theoretical and practical perspectives. It is a good idea, therefore, to begin your use of the Workbook by spending some time writing in response to at least four or five of the activities in this section, *before* moving on to tackle any of the activities in other sections.

All of these writing tasks present substantial challenges. It would not be realistic, or possible, to attempt all of them at one sitting. Some of these pieces of writing may be best tackled in short sections, adding new material on different occasions. It is possible that some of the writing tasks open up areas of memory and experience that are painful or unresolved. It may be right for you to wait until the right moment before embarking on these pieces of writing.

In any personal writing of this type, it can be helpful to create your own rituals and space within which you feel free to express yourself. Before you begin, you might wish to think about where and when would be best for you to do this kind of work.

Writing your autobiography: getting started

The purpose of this activity is to give you an opportunity to sketch the story of your life – your autobiography – in outline form. Being able to develop an understanding of your own development over time, and the ways in which you have responded to different external situations and demands, can be an invaluable resource for a counsellor. It can help to provide you with a means of understanding your own reactions to clients and of empathizing with the experiences and dilemmas that clients describe in relation to their own lives.

Instructions

Spend some time thinking about your life – its past, present and future. Imagine your life is like a book, with each of the major parts or stages comprising a chapter. Provide names for each of the chapters, and describe the content of each in a little more detail. What is the underlying theme of the book? Can you find a title for the story as a whole? Feel free to add anything else that seems relevant to constructing a framework for your autobiography. Remember – the purpose of this task is to facilitate *your* learning – go with what feels right for you.

As you are writing your autobiography, reflect on how it feels to write about yourself in this way. Are there some memories that are painful, which you would rather avoid? Are there other memories that are joyful and self-affirming?

You may find that, once you have started to write your autobiography, other episodes and themes come to mind. It may be valuable to add these to what you have written, so that you gradually build a more complete story of your life. It can often be useful to return to what you have written months or years later, and reflect on the ways in which you have 're-written' your personal history.

Painful gaps in autobiographical narratives are discussed in the section on adult attachment, pages 104–5 of *An Introduction to Counselling*. The experience of positive autobiographical moments is explored in pages 146–8 and 235–8.

Further reading

This activity draws on the work of the narrative psychologist Dan McAdams. A good introduction to the approach to autobiography developed by McAdams can be found in:

McAdams, D.P. (1993) *The Stories We Live By: Personal Myths and the Making of the Self*. New York: William Murrow.
McAdams, D.P. (2000) *The Person: An Integrated Introduction*. New York: Wiley.

Keeping a personal journal

Many counselling courses require students or trainees to keep personal learning diaries or journals. 'Journalling' is an excellent way to explore and reflect on experience, and integrate theory and practice. The learning journal also makes it possible to keep track of personal change and development, and to keep hold of new insights (by writing them down) rather than losing them through forgetting. There is also a lot of evidence that writing can in itself be therapeutic (at some point in the future you may want to suggest to some of your counselling clients that they might want to keep a personal journal). Learning how to use a learning journal can therefore be viewed as an opportunity to gain first-hand experience of a powerful therapeutic tool.

The learning journal can function not only as a place where you record your responses to the learning activities in this Workbook, but also as place to record and reflect on other learning experiences associated with becoming a counsellor, for example lectures, workshops, tutorials, supervision sessions and actual counselling sessions with clients.

Some suggestions for how to keep a Learning Journal:

1. Choose a medium that is right for you. This could be a notebook, a ring binder that you can add pages to, or a folder on your computer;

2. Keep it safe. You will not want other people to see what you have written unless you ask them to. Find a way of maintaining your privacy;

3. Date each entry in the journal and give it a title. This will help you to make sense of what you have written when you read it later;

4. Write quickly, as if you are allowing your 'stream of consciousness' to flow on to the page. Try not to censor what you write. Don't worry about spelling, punctuation or grammar – what you are writing is just for you;

5. Experiment with different ways of writing. Sometimes it is useful to write a list of ideas or images rather than attempting to produce continuous prose. Sometimes it may be helpful to draw pictures, use coloured pens, or construct diagrams.

6. Some people find it helpful to get into a routine or ritual where they write their journal at a particular time and place each day;

7. Other people find it helpful to keep notebooks or scraps of paper with them so that they can note down 'flashes' or sudden ideas and insights. Things can come to you when you are walking along a road, immediately when you wake up in the morning, or when you are in a meeting or lecture – times when you would not be able to write a 'proper' journal entry;

8. The learning journal is not a personal diary. It is focused on your involvement with the roles, tasks and challenges of being or becoming a counsellor. If very personal things come up for you, it may be sensible to write about them in a separate personal diary. It is not healthy to let 'being a counsellor' dominate your whole life.

Further reading

There are several sources that introduce different journal-writing techniques. Particularly recommended are:

Adams, K. (1990) *Journal to the Self*. New York: Warner Books.

Rainer, T. (1978) *The New Diary*. London: Angus and Robertson.

Rainer, T. (1997) *Your Life as Story: Writing the New Autobiography*. New York: G.P. Putnam.

Thompson, K. (2004) Journal writing as a therapeutic tool, in G. Bolton, S. Howlett, C. Lago and J. Wright (eds) *Writing Cures: An Introductory Handbook of Writing in Counselling and Psychotherapy*. London: Brunner-Routledge.

The story of a helping relationship

If you are to build on your own experience, then it is important to be aware of your own strengths and 'gifts' in counselling situations. Even if you have never taken on a formal counselling role, there will have been times in your life when you have been involved in helping someone else to talk through a personal problem. The aim of this exercise is to give you an opportunity to begin to reflect on what you already know, in relation to counselling – what are the skills and areas of awareness that you already possess?

This task requires writing about an occasion in which you were involved in a helping relationship with someone. The person you were helping could have been a counselling client, or a friend or family member. The helping relationship may be a formal one, in the context of your work, or an informal one, in the context of family or friends. Your task is to write an account of what happened when you helped this person. You should cover such questions as:

(?) What led up to the helping incident, what was the background to you being involved with the person in this way?

(?) What were your aims, what did you want to accomplish?

(?) What did you say and do?

(?) What was going on in your mind at every stage of the process?

(?) What did you feel about what you were doing?

(?) What was the outcome – how did it all end?

Your account of this incident should have a beginning, a middle and an end. Keep it descriptive of what actually happened and what you actually did and felt – there is no need to interpret or explain your actions for the purpose of the exercise. It is best if you choose an incident to write about where you felt you were reasonably successful in what you were trying to achieve. Do not include any identifying characteristics of the person being helped. Change their name and any other possible identifying features, just in case anyone else reads what you have written.

The event you select should be a reasonably complex incident, something that lets you express and explore your capacity to help. You can write as much or as little as seems right to you, but aim to reach at least 500 words. Give your story a title.

Later exercises in the Workbook invite you to look at what you have written from a variety of different theoretical perspectives.

Further reading

The work of Combs is briefly described on page 482 of *An Introduction to Counselling*.

This task is based on the work of Arthur Combs, who was an early colleague of Carl Rogers. Combs believed that helping relationship stories revealed a great deal about the values and attitudes of counsellors. Information about the research he carried out using this technique, and his approach to analysing such stories, can be found in:

Combs, A.W. (1986) What makes a good helper?, *Person-Centered Review*, 1:51–61.

Combs, A.W. (1990) *A Theory of Therapy. Guidelines for Counseling Practice*. London: Sage.

The origins and development of your interest in counselling

This activity gives you an opportunity to explore some of the meanings of being a counsellor that may have arisen from your life experience.

Instructions

Imagine yourself some time in the future, when you are established in your career as a counsellor. Imagine that you are in *your* counselling room. It is your *ideal* counselling room, furnished and decorated to create an optimal working environment for you. Look around it – what do you see? Now, imagine that three or four of your closest colleagues or friends in the counselling world are coming to visit you in this room. These are people who really know you, who understand and accept you. Who are they? Welcome them. They have come for a special reason, to hear you tell your story of how you became a counsellor. Think about becoming a counsellor as a journey. Start right at the beginning of that journey. Tell them about your earliest experiences in family and school that somehow seem connected to your choice of being a counsellor. Describe the people, places, relationships and events that have influenced you in the direction of counselling. Identify the choice points, where you made decisions to commit yourself more fully to this type of work. Bring the story up to date. Tell them where you have arrived on your 'counselling journey'.

You may find it useful to close your eyes for a few minutes and imagine telling this story. Then write it down. Try to write in as much detail as you can. Write quickly – don't censor what you put down. You may find that there are other bits of your story that occur to you over the next few days – add these in later. Remember, this is your personal story. There are no right or wrong answers, and no-one will see what you have written, unless you invite them to.

Suggestions for further reflection

You may find it helpful to think about the story you have written in terms of the section on *The Counsellor's Journey* (*An Introduction to Counselling*, pages 489–93). To what extent do you think that this model can help you to make sense of your experience of becoming a counsellor?

Your favourite story

Most of us have a story that, somehow, has a special appeal to us. This learning activity invites you to identify, then write down, your favourite story (Part 1), and then reflect on what you have written in terms of a series of prompt questions (Part 2).

Learning task

Identifying your favourite story:

➡ What is your favourite story? This could be a fairy tale, novel, short story, play, film, TV show and so on;

➡ Give a brief summary of the story, in your own words. It does not matter whether your version is different from the original – what matters is the story as *you* recall it. Write the story in as much vivid detail as you can.

Exploring the personal meaning of your favourite story

Slowly read through what you have written, and make notes in response to the following questions:

? Who is your favourite character in the story?

? Why do you like this character so much?

? What happens to this character?

? Who are the other characters? What kind of relationship does your favourite character have with these other characters?

? What is the setting for the story? Where does it take place?

? What is the main feeling tone of the story?

? When did you first come across this story? How often, and in what ways, do you refresh your acquaintance with this story?

? Why do you like this particular story? Why do you think that you chose it? Are there other stories that you might have selected instead?

Finally – give yourself some time to reflect on what you have learned about yourself from this process.

Some suggestions for exploring the meaning of stories, such as a favourite story, are provided in the learning activity *Making sense of stories*, in Section 4 of the Workbook.

The self puzzle

Most approaches to counselling emphasize the importance, in one way or another, of the person's sense of *self*. The notion of an individual self, as the core of who a person feels himself or herself to be, lies at the heart of psychology and psychotherapy.

There are many different ways of understanding or picturing the self. Sigmund Freud, for example, portrayed the self as similar to an iceberg, with the largest part beneath the surface.

In order to engage with a client's sense of self, it is usual to have an appreciation of your own sense of self. This activity introduces a simple method for beginning to explore the way that the self is structured and organized.

The exercise requires access to coloured pens or crayons, and a piece of blank paper (a large piece of paper is best). The task is to draw a map or puzzle, to represent the way you view your self, following these guidelines:

In some ways everyone is a puzzle, consisting of many different parts. You are a puzzle with parts that are unique to you. Draw a puzzle with parts that are labelled that best describe you, as you see yourself now. The number of parts, the shape of the parts, and the positioning of the parts are all up to you. They should, however, be used to represent yourself as descriptively as possible. There are no right and wrong answers. This self puzzle is your own creation – take as long as you wish to complete it. An alternative way of thinking about this creation is to look at it as a map. Similarly, the map of how you see yourself now will include areas that are labelled.

The importance for counsellors of developing accurate self-awareness is highlighted on pages 501–3 of An *Introduction to Counselling*. Different ways of understanding the idea of *self* are discussed on pages 30 and 286–7.

Be aware of the thoughts and feelings that accompany this task, as you construct your puzzle or map. After you have made the map, it may be helpful to write some notes about these thoughts and feelings, and also of what you have learned about yourself through engaging in this activity.

Once you have completed this exercise, you may find it useful to turn to the *Making sense of self* learning task in Section 2 of the Workbook, which includes some guidelines for interpreting your self puzzle picture.

Further reading

The idea of the self puzzle has been adapted from Loo, C.M. (1974) The self-puzzle. A diagnostic and therapeutic tool, *Journal of Personality*, 42:236–42.

Thickening your autobiography: early memories

This exercise provides an opportunity to carry out some further exploration around the complexity and richness of your understanding of who you are – your autobiography. Many clients who seek therapy can be viewed as engaged in a struggle to achieve a coherent appreciation of many different, and often difficult, strands of their life experience. To be able to facilitate this kind of meaning-making, it is invaluable to have undergone such a process yourself.

The idea that 'thin' life stories are restricting of possibilities, whereas 'thick' stories enable a wider variety of options to be pursued, is taken from the writings of Michael White, one of the founders of narrative therapy. See pages 234–40 of *An Introduction to Counselling*.

Attachment theory offers a valuable framework for making sense of early memories. See pages 100–6 of *An Introduction to Counselling*.

Early memories can often represent a highly significant source of meaning in a person's life. Take some time to identify, then write down, your earliest memories. Describe the memories in as much detail as possible. Begin by going back to your childhood and try to recall your *earliest* childhood memory. Try to recall a specific incident or event, not just a fragmentary impression. What are your impressions of yourself, and of each of the other people in the memory? Describe, also, the mood or feeling tone that goes with this memory.

Once you have written about your earliest memory, you may find it useful to explore other early memories, for example, your first memory of your mother, father, siblings or other family members, or memories of moments that were high points, or formative turning points, in your life.

When reflecting on what you have written about your early memories, it is helpful to ask yourself whether the pattern of needs, relationships and emotions that are represented in these stories have persisted as themes in your life. It can also be instructive to share your early memories with other people. What does it feel like to tell another person about these memories? What impact does this telling have on your relationship with that person?

Further reading

The importance of early memories was first recognized by Alfred Adler, one of Freud's inner circle. The specific early memory instructions used in this exercise are derived from research carried out by Martin Mayman and his colleagues. Further information on these studies can be found in:

Fowler, J.C., Hilsenroth, M.J. and Handler, L. (2000) Martin Mayman's early memories technique: bridging the gap between personality assessment and psychotherapy, *Journal of Personality Assessment*, 75:18–32.

Mayman, M. (1968) Early memories and character structure, *Journal of Projective Techniques & Personality Assessment*, 32:303–16.

Mayman, M. and Faris, M. (1960) Early memories as expressions of relationship paradigms, *American Journal of Orthopsychiatry*, 30:507–20.

Many other researchers and therapists have explored the notion that early memories convey, in summary form, the key existential themes that influence the directions of a person's life:

Csikzentmihalyi, M. and Beattie, O. (1979) Life themes: a theoretical and empirical exploration of their origins and effects, *Journal of Humanistic Psychology*, 19:45–63.

McAdams, D.P., Hoffman, B.J., Mansfield, E.D. and Day, R. (1996) Themes of agency and communion in significant autobiographical scenes, *Journal of Personality*, 64:339–77.

An excellent summary of different approaches to working with early memories in therapy is:

Clark, A. (2002) *Early Recollections: Theory and Practice in Counseling and Psychotherapy*. New York: Brunner-Routledge.

Sexualities and counselling relationships

The meaning and importance of sexuality in everyday life, and in counselling, is a topic that counsellors need to be able to explore with clients. In psychoanalytic and psychodynamic approaches to counselling and psychotherapy, sexuality is explicitly theorized, through constructs such as 'libido'. In 'gay affirmative' therapy, it is recommended that sexual orientation should be openly, and acceptantly, discussed. In much couple counselling, the issue of sexual relationships and sexual satisfaction is often a central focus of the therapy. Even in approaches to therapy, or with individual clients, where sexuality is not specifically emphasized, there will be times when this issue is highlighted.

The aim of this activity is to provide a structure within which your experience of sexuality can be explored, and the implications for your approach to counselling can be identified.

Over the next two or three days, give yourself some time to engage in an inquiry into your sexuality. The following suggestions may help to get you started:

1. How has your sexuality developed? Draw a 'timeline', stretching from birth to the present, and enter the key events and stages/phases in the growth of your sexual awareness and behaviour;

2. Where does sexuality fit into your life? What part does it play? How do you use your sexual awareness and energy?

3. What are your attitudes and feelings in relation to people whose sexual orientation and behaviour differs from your own?

4. Describe how you have dealt with (or anticipate that you would deal with) a counselling relationship where:
   a. You felt sexually attracted to the person you were helping
   b. The person you were helping expressed sexual attraction towards you
   How did you (or might you) respond in each case?

5. How would you react to a client who asked you to help him or her make sense of, and resolve, a sexual problem? Which sexual problems would you feel more/less confident in working with? What would you do if you did not feel confident or competent to work with the client in the way that he or she had requested?

Once you have written and reflected around these questions (and possibly around other questions or themes that may have struck you as interesting in this area), then shift to consideration of the implications of what you have discovered, for your sense of who you are as a counsellor. For example, do you feel that you need to acquire more knowledge about sexuality? Is your approach to sexuality consistent with the assumptions of your preferred theoretical model?

> Issues around sexuality in therapy are discussed on pages 80–2, 402–7 and 520–1 of *An Introduction to Counselling*.

Further reading

Davies, D. and Neal, C. (eds) (1996) *Pink Therapy: A Guide for Counsellors and Therapists Working with Gay, Lesbian and Bisexual Clients*. Buckingham: Open University Press.

Rutter, P. (1989) *Sex in the Forbidden Zone*. London: Mandala.

Your personal experience of counselling

One of the consistent themes in all approaches to counsellor training is that it is important for helpers to know what it is like to be the *recipient* of help. The aim of this activity is to encourage you to focus on your experience of being helped, and to reflect on the implications of that experience for your understanding of the helping process.

Instructions

How do qualified therapists describe their experience of personal therapy? See pages 486–7 of *An Introduction to Counselling*.

What is your own personal experience of receiving counselling, either on a formal, contracted basis or informally from a friend, teacher or priest (or anyone else who is not a member of your immediate family)? Write a brief account of one useful or successful 'counselling' encounter that you have experienced. Make sure you write your story in a place that is private and confidential, so you can be as open and honest as possible.

You may find the following questions useful in terms of structuring your account:

- What was troubling you?
- At what stage of your life did this trouble emerge?
- What made you seek help, or be open to receiving help, at this particular point?
- How did you make contact with this 'helper'?
- What happened during the 'counselling' or 'helping' session or sessions?
- What were the most useful things your 'counsellor' did?
- Was there anything unhelpful that he/she did?
- How did this 'counselling' help you, what was the long term impact on you?

Next, if possible, write a parallel account of a counselling/helping episode (again, where you were the recipient of help) that was *not* helpful.

Reflect on what you have learned from this task, especially in terms of: the aims of counselling (pages 12–13 of *An Introduction to Counselling*), the process of counselling (Chapter 13), and the qualities of the effective counsellor (Chapter 19).

What you bring to counselling

For many people, the decision to become a counsellor or psychotherapist may follow a period of time studying, and working in, another profession or discipline, such as nursing, social work, teaching, the ministry or psychology. These early-career activities may shape the way that people are viewed, and 'helping' or 'therapy' are understood. Some trainees or students on counselling courses find that, at the beginning of their training, they have a tendency to look at issues through the lens or perspective of their primary profession. Others may be so highly motivated to leave their primary profession behind that they deny its relevance to their work as a counsellor.

This worksheet invites you to reflect on *what you bring to counselling*, in terms of previous knowledge, skills and experience. The following questions are intended to focus your exploration of this issue:

> The interdisciplinary nature of counselling is discussed on pages 13–14 of *An Introduction to Counselling*.
>
> The idea of the 'counsellor's journey' is explored on pages 489–93.

 Divide a page into two columns. In the left column, list all of the potential areas of your life experience that may be sources of knowledge, skills and experience that may be relevant to counselling. These could be jobs you have done (e.g. worked as an emergency room nurse for two years) or they could be linked to your family or personal life (e.g. 'my mother and father divorced when I was 10 years old').

 In the right column, list the knowledge, skills and experience that you acquired as a result of the life experiences that you have identified. For example, 'working as an emergency room nurse' may have helped you to 'understand how people behave in crisis' and to 'talk openly about death'. The divorce of your parents may have enabled you to 'be sensitive to the effect that loss of attachments in childhood can have on the rest of a person's life'.

 What have you brought with you from your previous experience that might be a strength or asset in relation to your work as a counsellor?

 What have you brought with you that might be a hindrance or distraction? Examples: 'the "nurse" part of me wants to solve people's problems for them', 'studying academic psychology encouraged me to be objective and detached, rather than empathic'.

 Some people find that counselling training seems to cut them off from what they already knew, in a practical sense, about helping others. Michael White (1997: 13) has described this process in these terms:

…entry into the culture of psychotherapy is associated with an induction in which the more local or folk knowledges that have been generated in a person's history are marginalised, often disqualified, and displaced by the formal and expert knowledges of the professional disciplines, and by a shift in what counts in regard to the significant memberships of a person's life. In this process the monoculture of psychotherapy is substituted for the diverse, historical and local associations of persons' lives.

To what extent have you been aware of this process taking place with respect to your own involvement in counselling training and practice?

Becoming a counsellor can be viewed as a journey, which takes several years and on which many challenges must be faced. What are the tools and skills that you take with you on this journey, and how best can they be used?

Further reading

The experiences of counsellors and psychotherapists who have found ways to use their earlier work and study (in a wide range of professions and disciplines) to inform their therapy practice, are described in:

Thome, B. and Dryden, W. (eds) (1993) *Counselling: Interdisciplinary Perspectives.* Buckingham: Open University Press.

Exploring cultural identity

A sense of personal identity and belonging, of values and image of the 'good life', is rooted in the culture in which we live. Culture makes us who we are:

> ...we enter human society ... with one or more imputed characters – roles into which we have been drafted – and we have to learn what they are in order to understand how others respond to us and how our responses to them are apt to be construed (MacIntyre, 1981: 216)

When we meet someone else, we immediately begin to de-code all the cues relating to their cultural position – social class, gender, ethnicity, race, religion, sexual orientation, political affiliation and so on. At the same time, the other person is doing the same with us.

In counselling, it is necessary to be aware of the various strands of your cultural identity. This helps you to:

> Be aware of the kind of impact you might be having on the other person;

> Appreciate the cultural roots of the theory/model you are using;

> Be sensitive to and curious about the other person's cultural identity;

> Talk about cultural difference when this becomes relevant within the counselling relationship;

> Appreciate the impact of social class, religion and other cultural factors in the life of the client;

> Defuse your fear of the other.

The aim of this activity is to help you to become aware of your cultural identity.

> Key dimensions of cultural identity are discussed in *An Introduction to Counselling*, pages 244–54. An example of a genogram can be found on pages 195–6.

Instructions

1. Very quickly, without thinking too much about it, write down a list of your first 20 answers to the question 'Who am I?'. What does this list tell you about your cultural identity?

2. What are the different sources and strands of your cultural identity? Write out a genogram, or 'family tree', indicating beside each person (parents, grandparents, great grandparents) the information you have about their cultural and social position. What does this genogram tell you about your cultural identity: to what extent are these cultural themes influential in your life now?

3. What kind of cultural exploration have you carried out within your life? What new cultural influences have you been exposed to, or sought out? Draw a 'lifeline' from birth until now, and indicate on it the significant cultural shifts that you can recall. For example, have you moved away from, or towards, any of the cultural traditions represented by people depicted in your genogram? What new people or institutions have come into your life, bringing different cultural influences?

4. What is the meaning of 'home' for you? Where is the place you belong? (Home can be imaginary or real.)

Finally – reflect on, and write about, what you have learned about your cultural identity. How might you describe and sum up your cultural identity, if you were invited to work with a group of colleagues from another culture?

Further reading

McGoldrick, M. (1998) Belonging and liberation: finding a place called 'home', in M. McGoldrick (ed.) *Re-visioning Family Therapy: Race, Culture and Gender in Clinical Practice*. New York: Guilford Press.

Feeling really understood

Descriptions of the impact of being empathically understood can be found on page 173 of *An Introduction to Counselling*.

At the heart of counselling is the hope that someone else can accept and understand us for who were are, without judgement or analysis. The aim of this exercise is to encourage you to explore the significance, in your own life, of this type of moment.

Instructions

Sit quietly for a few seconds...

Think about the *last time you felt really accepted and understood by another person.*

Once you have identified such an occasion, you should briefly describe (on a piece of paper):

➡ What the circumstances were;

➡ How you felt;

➡ What the consequences or effects of being accepted and understood were.

Following this piece of writing take some time to reflect on the implications of the experience of being understood for your approach as a counsellor.

Further reading

A research study which has analysed the experience of being understood is:

Bachelor, A. (1988) How clients perceive therapist empathy: a content analysis of 'received' empathy, *Psychotherapy*, 25:227–40.

You may find it interesting to look at how your own experience compares with what was reported by participants in this investigation.

Mapping your relationship patterns

The aim of this activity is to give you an opportunity to explore the different types of relationships you have had with other people at various times in your life.

Instructions

Take some pens and blank pieces of paper and make some simple diagrams that map out your relationships with the people who have been important to you at different stages in your life. It is best to draw each diagram on a separate piece of paper. In the middle of the page, you should draw a circle to represent yourself. Write 'me' or your name inside this circle. Around yourself, you should arrange the people who were important for you at that point in your life. The distance from you on the page should be used to represent their emotional, psychological or inner presence for you, rather than who was physically there, how far away they lived, or similar factors.

What you will end up with is like a map of the planets, with a set of circles around a central 'star'. Please label each circle with the name of the person who belongs there.

There are two additional kinds of circles that you might find yourself wanting to draw. One is a 'dotted circle' to indicate someone who mattered a lot to you at that time of your life but who was not there at all as a physical presence. This might be someone whom you talked to in your head or thought about a lot even though you had no real connection with him or her at that time.

Another kind of circle you might like to draw is a group circle. This you might draw to indicate people who were important as a group but didn't really matter as individuals. This might be important, for instance, if you wanted to indicate the importance of a sports team or church group or something like that.

Draw these diagrams starting at age five, then at 10-year intervals up to the present. They will go better if you think of yourself at these particular ages rather than trying to do the years in between. So, imagine yourself at age five, try to fix yourself in time, and then pretend to interview yourself, asking about who is in your mind at that time. Then imagine yourself at age 15, 25, and so on up to your present age.

Once you have completed your diagrams, reflect on the following questions:

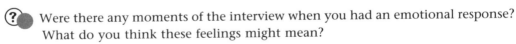 Were there any moments of the interview when you had an emotional response? What do you think these feelings might mean?

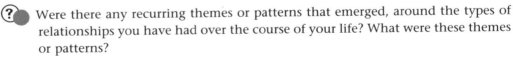 Were there any recurring themes or patterns that emerged, around the types of relationships you have had over the course of your life? What were these themes or patterns?

(?) What might be some of the implications of your relationship style, for your work as a counsellor? How might the ways of relating that run through your life have an impact on your counselling? What kinds of relationships are you more likely to have with clients, colleagues, tutors/trainers and supervisors?

Further reading

This activity is adapted from: Josselson, R. (1996) *The Space between Us: Exploring the Dimensions of Human Relationships*. Thousand Oaks, CA: Sage. This book also provides a very useful framework for making sense of relationship patterns.

Engaging with difference

As a counsellor, you may have little choice in relation to the characteristics of the people who use your service. Many people who seek your help will undoubtedly be easy to like, understandable, admirable. These are people with whom you may feel comfortable and enjoy an easy rapport. But there will be some service users who, for you, are difficult. These are people who make you feel far from comfortable, in whose presence you feel threatened, on edge, lost.

The purpose of this exercise is to explore the theme of *difference* in your life. Give yourself some time to reflect on, and write about, your responses to the following questions:

(?) Which groups of people do you regard as being *most different* from you? Make a list;

(?) Beside each group, write a set of adjectives that you might use to describe what they are like;

(?) Generate another set of adjectives, to capture how you imagine you might feel in the presence of a member of this group;

(?) What are the sources of your information about each of these groups of people? How much of your information is first hand, arising from personal contact, and how much from other sources? How much curiosity do you have about each of these groups?

Looking at what you have written, can you identify any themes in your responses? What lies at the heart of *difference*, for you? Is difference a matter of values, gender, social class, race, physical appearance? What is it that makes someone different? Can you make connections between these meanings of difference, for you, and other aspects of your biography?

In relation to your work as a counsellor, imagine for a few moments who your least-preferred client might be. How would you react, and what would you do, if this client walked into your counselling room?

Finally, what is your personal experience of *being different*? What are the situations in your own life in which you have felt as though you did not 'fit in', were not accepted by others, or did not 'know the rules'? What are your strategies for coping with such situations? How can you use your own experience of *being different* to inform your work as a counsellor?

> The issue of difference is explored in Chapter 14 of *An Introduction to Counselling*.

Further reading

The essential role of curiosity in dissolving difference is discussed in: Dyche, L. and Zayas, L.H. (1995) The value of curiosity and naivete for the cross-cultural psychotherapist, *Family Process*, 34:389–99.

A valuable collection of papers on the theme of identity and difference in therapy is: McGoldrick, M. (ed.) (1998) *Re-visioning Family Therapy: Race, Culture and Gender in Clinical Practice*. New York: Guilford Press.

How do you cope with crisis in your own life?

The majority of people who use counselling do so in response to an immediate crisis. Even if a person has lived with difficulties for a considerable time, there is typically a particular event which triggers the decision to seek outside help. In order to appreciate what a person might be experiencing when they contact a counselling agency with a problem, it is useful to reflect on your own personal experience of crisis.

Instructions

Write about your experience of a crisis in your own life, within the framework provided by the following questions:

1. Briefly describe an episode in your life when you felt that you had reached a real crisis point as a result of a problem such as work pressure, the demands on you as a carer, feeling depressed or hopeless, feeling really worried, feeling panic in particular situations, feeling traumatized after an accident or assault and so on;

2. How was your capacity to cope affected during the worst points in this episode? Briefly describe the impact of the situation on your capacity to make decisions, take care of yourself, control your emotions, and 'think straight';

3. What helped you to get through this? Describe how you used both your own personal resources (e.g. humour, courage, spirituality) and other people's to help you to cope;

4. How long did it take you to work through this crisis?

5. What was the most difficult aspect of the crisis?

6. What helped you most?

7. What have you learned about yourself, and other people, as a result of this event? How have you changed?

Further reading

James, R. and Gilliland, B. (2001) *Crisis Intervention Strategies*. Belmont, CA: Wadsworth.

Kanel, K. (1999) *A Guide to Crisis Intervention*. Belmont, CA: Wadsworth.

The experience of changing your own behaviour

Think of an occasion when you were able to change your own behaviour, in what you considered to be a positive direction. This should be an occasion when you intentionally planned to make a change in your behaviour, and carried it through to completion. If it is not possible for you to identify a time when you were successful in changing your behaviour, then write about an episode in which you made an attempt to do so.

Instructions

Take a few moments to identify an unwanted habit or behaviour pattern that you have managed to eliminate or minimize in your life, or to establish a new pattern. The unwanted behaviour could be something like smoking, eating chocolate, arguing, being late or anything else that you have wanted to change in yourself. A desired new behaviour could be something like taking more exercise, spending quality time with your family, or tidying up your room.

Describe what happened:

(?) What was the behaviour you decided to change?

(?) Why was this pattern of behaviour a problem for you?

(?) Had you tried – unsuccessfully – to change this habit before? Why had you been unsuccessful?

(?) What did you do to enable the change to take place this time?

(?) What helped you in making these changes?

(?) What hindered you?

(?) Did you experience any setbacks or relapses? How did you overcome them?

(?) What did you learn about yourself, and about how you would set about changing things if you need to again in the future?

> The theory of relapse prevention is introduced on page 139 of *An Introduction to Counselling*.

Finally, reflecting on what you have written, what are the implications of the episode you have described here for the way in which you understand change to take place in counselling? To what extent does your experience of changing your behaviour generalize to a counselling situation?

The role of therapy in your life-story

People who seek counselling or psychotherapy are often stuck at a point of choice in their lives, faced with a dilemma over choices to make. To appreciate what this is like, it is helpful to be able to draw upon an understanding of your own experience of making important life choices.

Instructions

Take a blank sheet of paper and a pen.

Staring with the year of your birth, draw a line to the first choice juncture that you can think of. Show that the path forks, giving you a number of alternatives. Which path did you take? Make sure to indicate the paths *not taken*, as well as the one that you did take. The choices should be ones that had an important effect on your life. When you have finished with one choice point, go on to the next one. Note your age at each choice point, and give each of the paths (taken and untaken) a brief label. Continue until you reach your present age.

Figure 1 provides an illustration of the kind of choice map that you might generate:

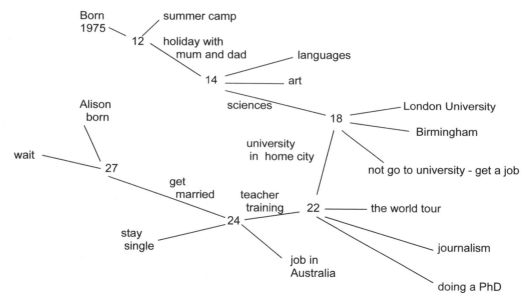

My life choices. Andy Simpson, August 2003

Reflecting on your choice map

Looking at your map as a whole, what patterns and themes do you see? Is there any consistency to the paths you have *not* chosen? What has your involvement with therapy been around these choice points in your life? To what extent, and in what ways, has therapy facilitated your life decisions?

Further reading

The choices in life exercise has been adapted from the following paper:

Lewchanin, S. and Zubrod, L.A. (2001) Choices in life: a clinical tool for facilitating midlife review, *Journal of Adult Development*, 8:193–6.

How relevant is spirituality?

The emergence of counselling and psychotherapy in the mid-twentieth century, as widely available forms of psychological care, was associated with an emphasis on a rational, scientific world view that allowed little place for spirituality and religious experience. However, more recently, influential figures in the therapy profession have called for a re-integration of spiritual experience into counselling theory and practice:

Our experiences in therapy, and in groups, it is clear, involve the transcendent, the indescribable, the spiritual. I am compelled to believe that I, like many others, have under-estimated the importance of this mystical, spiritual realm. (Rogers, 1980 p. 124)

My own belief ... is that anyone who wants to be a good psychotherapist has to have their own spiritual discipline which they follow. (Rowan, 1993 p. 47)

What place does spirituality have within your approach as a counsellor? Consider the following questions:

The relationship between therapy and religion is discussed on pages 21 and 28 of *An Introduction to Counselling*.

 What is your relationship with spirituality? What does spirituality mean for you?

 In what ways do you (or might you wish to) draw upon spiritual practices (e.g. prayer, meditation, yoga, reading, use of sacred objects) in preparing yourself for, or coping with the demands of, counselling work?

What types of spiritual experience have you encountered in your life? Have any of these experiences taken place during counselling or similar work? What do you understand these experiences to signify?

Where do spiritual and religious factors fit into your theoretical approach?

Further reading

West, W. (2000) *Psychotherapy and Spirituality*. London: Sage.

How do you cope under pressure?

Being a counsellor requires a capacity to be a companion to other people at their times of greatest anguish, despair or rage. In talking about the importance of each counsellor developing an approach that is firmly based in their own personal way of being, Peter Lomas (1999) has argued that:

...the business [of therapy] is to do with finding their own way, using their own intuition, learning to be themselves in the presence of someone who is asking for help, who is probably putting all kinds of pressures on them. (p. 25)

How have you responded in the past when someone with whom you have a relationship of care puts emotional pressure on you? Describe and explore the ways in which you have responded to the following life events:

⇒ Someone who is close to you is terminally ill;

⇒ You are on your own looking after a baby or young child who will not stop crying;

⇒ You are with a child or teenager who has a tantrum because he or she cannot get what they want;

⇒ Someone you care about has received news of a loss;

⇒ Someone you care about is hurt;

⇒ A person in your family has a 'breakdown', talks in ways that do not make sense, and declares that he or she is going away to end it all.

These are all very difficult situations, that can evoke a wide spectrum of feelings in a helper or companion. What has your emotional response been in these situations? What have you *done* – have you moved closer, retreated, withdrawn, displaced your concern into other behaviour? How has the quality of your connection with the other person changed or shifted at these moments?

Once you have mapped out your way of reacting to these demanding situations in everyday life, take some time to reflect on the potential implications of what you have learned for your work as a counsellor.

Do you have a preferred learning style?

Different people learn in different ways. For example, some people gain more from reading and individual reflection, while others learn better when actively doing things with others. The model of *experiential learning* developed by David Kolb suggests that the process of learning consists of four phases. For instance, if a person is interested in learning how to perform a task more effectively, the following processes can be observed:

➡ *Concrete Experience* occurs when the person is involved in carrying out a task;

➡ *Reflection* on that experience, on a personal basis – a process of individual sense-making;

➡ *Abstract Conceptualization* is a phase that involves identifying general rules describing the experience, or the application of known theories to it, which leads to ideas about ways of modifying the next occurrence of the experience;

➡ *Active Experimentation* represents the application of these new skills or ideas in practice, which in turn leads to a new set of concrete experiences, which are then in turn reflected on.

This sequence of learning steps may take place within a few minutes, or may extend over months, depending on the topic. Kolb, and other researchers, have noted that although any competent learner will have the capacity to function in each of these ways, individuals tend to grow up specializing in one or two 'preferred' learning processes. The theory of personal learning styles devised by Peter Honey is based on four primary learning styles, which correspond to the four phases of Kolb's cyclical model:

1️⃣ Activists involve themselves fully in doing things, enjoy team work, and eagerly embrace opportunities for practical, experiential activities. They are open to new learning experiences;

2️⃣ Reflectors prefer to stand back and look at experiences from many different perspectives. They collect data and prefer to think about it thoroughly before coming to any conclusions;

3️⃣ Theorists adapt and integrate observations into complex but logically sound theories. They are interested in concepts and think problems through in a step-by-step, logical way;

4️⃣ Pragmatists are keen to try out ideas, theories and techniques to see if they work in practice. They positively search out new ideas and take the first opportunity to experiment with applications.

A preference for any one of these learning styles is likely to mean that a person will be frustrated with learning experiences that are based on a different model. For example, activists may become impatient with theory and precise instructions, while theorists may be uncomfortable with the messiness and ambiguity of many practical situations.

Learning task

What are the implications of your learning style for your personal approach as a counsellor? Consider the following questions:

(?) How do you define your learning style?

(?) In what ways does your preferred style of learning explain your level of interest and enthusiasm in different types of learning within your counsellor training (for example, reading about theory, participating in a personal development group, being an observer in skills practice sessions)?

(?) What are the links between your preferred learning style and the theoretical approach(es) with which you most identify?

(?) Could your way of working with clients, within an actual counselling session, be viewed as an expression of your learning style? Do you create certain kinds of learning opportunities for clients, and not others?

(?) How sensitive are you to the learning styles of other people? How well do you respond to the learning process of clients who have learning styles different from your own?

Further reading

Honey, P. and Mumford, A. (2000) *The Learning Styles Questionnaire*. Maidenhead: Peter Honey Learning.

Kolb, D.A. (1984) *Experiential Learning: Experience as the Source of Learning and Development*. Englewood Cliffs, NJ: Prentice-Hall.

A number of self-test learning styles inventories are available on the internet.

What motivates you?

This task is linked to the discussion of the *counsellor's journey* on pages 489–93 of *An Introduction to Counselling.*

How important are each of these sources of motivation for you in your counselling work? Place a '1' beside the most important, '2' for the second most important and so on. Add any additional sources of motivation that come to mind.

➡ Contact with other people (clients) in a controlled situation;

➡ Discovery – learning about human beings;

➡ Social status and respect;

➡ Payment, making a living;

➡ Helping or healing others;

➡ Being powerful and having an impact on clients;

➡ Self-therapy, learning about myself through the work;

➡ Vicarious experience, the interest of learning about other people's lives;

➡ Feeling wanted and needed;

➡ Because I received therapy myself and want to 'give something back';

➡ Doing a job that is intellectually challenging.

Once you have rank ordered these sources of motivation, consider the following questions:

? How open are you with other people, such as colleagues, about your motivation to do this work? There may be sources of motivation that you conceal for others – what difference would it make to own up to these factors?

? How do these sources of motivation/satisfaction influence and shape the way you work, for example the decisions you make about the kind of work that you do?

? How have your acquired these motives – where do they come from in your life? For example, are there experiences in childhood, or significant people you have met, that you can recognize as representing the origins of these motives?

? How sustainable are these factors? Can you anticipate any of them becoming less motivating for you? What would you do if this happened?

Reflecting on the experience of writing about yourself

The activities in this section of the Workbook have invited you to write about many different aspects of your personal life. The technique of personal writing has been used by many therapists as a way of helping clients. For example, the task of writing about a problem was used by the American psychologist James Pennebaker in a series of experiments where people were asked to write for a period of around 20 minutes each day for four days. Pennebaker found that writing about difficult experiences was painful at the time, but in the end helpful (even bringing about improvements in physical health). His work has been very influential and he has generated a useful model of the psychologically damaging effects of inhibition and self-control in relation to problematic experiences.

In reflecting on your experience of writing about yourself, consider the following questions:

? What impact has this experience had on you? Has it been helpful to write about yourself, or unhelpful?

? What are the ways in which writing has been useful or otherwise for you?

? What have been the differences that you have noticed, between talking about an issue or experience, and writing about it?

? In what circumstances might you use writing activities with clients?

The therapeutic writing tasks used by Pennebaker focused on specific stressful events, while the writing exercises in the Workbook have encouraged you to explore key moments in your personal autobiography.

In relation to the autobiographical dimension of these writing activities, it may be useful to reflect on questions such as:

? What effects have you noticed, in terms of your feelings about your life, that have arisen from your autobiographical writing?

? How does (or could) a full and rich understanding of your own biography or life history help you in your work with clients?

The psychoanalyst John Bowlby suggested that emotional *attachments* to significant others represent the anchor points of an individual's life. Recent developments within attachment theory have included the construction of the *Adult Attachment Interview (AAI)* as a structured approach to exploring these anchor points within the story that a person tells of their life. A summary of these ideas is provided on pages 100–6 of *An Introduction to Counselling*.

In reflecting on attachment theory, and its relevance for your development as a counsellor, consider the following questions:

? To what extent do the patterns of attachment yielded by the AAI help you to make sesne of your own autobiography?

? In what ways could the *AAI* questions on page 104 facilitate further exploration of important aspects of your life-story?

How useful could this framework be in your work with clients? How could you make use of it?

Further reading

Bolton, G., Howlett, S., Lago, C. and Wright, J.K. (eds) (2004) *Writing Cures: An Introductory Handbook of Writing in Counselling and Psychotherapy.* London: Brunner-Routledge.

McAdams, D.P. (1993) *The Stories We Live By: Personal Myths and the Making of the Self.* New York: William Murrow.

Pennebaker, J. (1997) *Opening Up: The Healing Power of Expressing Emotions.* New York: Guilford Press.

Making sense: constructing a framework for understanding

The idea of the unconscious

What brings about change? The relative importance of cognition and emotion

Behind the theory: the life of the theorist

The cultural context of understanding

What kind of therapeutic relationship?

Dialogue between theorists

Are you postmodern?

Letter to a theorist

The concept of transference

Introduction

The work of a counsellor inevitably involves listening to people talk in detail about complex situations in their lives. Often, the person's way of telling his or her life story may be halting, incoherent, or punctuated by strong emotion. Almost always, there will be gaps in the story – things not said, things that may be too embarrassing or shameful to share with another person. Listening to such stories, in a context in which you are expected to do something to help, can be a confusing and overwhelming experience. Where to start? What does all this information mean? What can I say or do to make things better?

Theory provides a framework for understanding, a preliminary map of the territory that might be explored, a set of suggestions for possible directions of travel. It is one of the core tasks of any counsellor to find a theoretical 'home'. Some therapists prefer to develop membership of a coherent theoretical community, centred around one of the main approaches to therapy, such as psychodynamic, person-centred or CBT (Cognitive Behavioural Therapy). Other practitioners choose to follow a more integrative or eclectic path. In either case, it is essential to become thoroughly familiar with the theoretical constructs and language that one decides to use. All of the big, important concepts within therapy theory – the unconscious, the self, cognitive schema – can be understood or interpreted in different ways, and have multiple meanings and implications according to the circumstances in which they are used. Possessing a superficial understanding of such ideas can lead a counsellor into difficulties, for example if a client realizes that their therapist is only pretending to understand, is hiding behind technical jargon, or is contradicting herself or himself.

The activities in this section of the Workbook are designed to approach the goal of *making sense and constructing a framework for understanding* in a variety of ways. These activities invite you to:

➡ Reflect on the role of theory in counselling practice;

➡ Explore your own 'personal theories' and how these fit with the counselling models you have encountered;

➡ Look back at the implicit theoretical assumptions expressed in the writing you did in the *building on life experience* section of the Workbook;

➡ Examine key concepts in depth.

The role of theory in counselling is discussed on pages 42–52 of *An Introduction to Counselling*.

Throughout these learning activities, you are encouraged to build up a sense of your own personal framework for understanding. Many of the tasks ask you to identify your own *position* in relation to the theoretical ideas that you are exploring. The rationale for this is that your own personal framework for understanding is always *more than* any single theory of therapy can provide. Responding to people in crisis always involves drawing upon your life experience and common sense, as well as your knowledge of therapy models. It is important, therefore, to know *where you stand* in relation to the theoretical traditions that inform your work.

Later sections in the Workbook build on your exploration of theory, for example in applying it to understand individual cases, or to resolve practice issues. Finally, some of the exercises in Section 5 of this Workbook give you opportunities to integrate or sum up your theoretical position.

Although the activities in this section are cross-referenced to relevant pages in *An Introduction to Counselling*, an adequate appreciation of theoretical issues will usually require extensive further study of primary sources.

What does a counselling theory need to be able to do?

If you read between the lines of most counselling, psychotherapy and personality textbooks, you will find that there is a set of core questions, related to the basic processes of counselling, that any theoretical model needs to be able to answer. These questions include:

(?) What are the causes of people's problems?

(?) What are the main mechanisms and processes of change? What changes? How?

(?) What is the role of the counsellor? What is the optimal type of counsellor-client relationship? Why is the relationship important? Why is it necessary to have a strong 'therapeutic alliance'?

(?) What are the criteria for success and failure in counselling? What are the goals of therapy?

(?) What is the relative importance, in terms of making sense of clients' problems and the process of counselling, of: (a) cultural factors (including social class, ethnicity and gender); (b) cognition; (c) emotion; (d) biological/genetic factors?

How do you answer these questions? Which specific concepts and models, and broader theoretical traditions, do you draw upon? Which theoretical ideas and concepts appear in your answers to these questions? Do these concepts all derive from a single theoretical model, or do your answers contain a mix of ideas?

The nature of theories of therapy is explored in Chapter 3 of *An Introduction to Counselling*.

You may find it helpful to use a large sheet or roll of paper to map out your thinking in relation to these key theoretical questions. Be aware that what you produce will almost inevitably be complex and incomplete – many of the ways that practitioners think about issues such as the causes of problems are implicit and unexamined, and may emerge only in response to particular cases.

Once you have constructed your concept map, you may find it valuable to read pages 43–5 of *An Introduction to Counselling* and think about which of your concepts are core philosophical assumptions, which are observational shorthand 'labels', and which are actual theoretical propositions.

What is your relationship with theory?

The famous social psychologist Kurt Lewin, once said: 'There is nothing as practical as a good theory' (Marrow, 1977).

Do you agree? How important is theory for you? Are you interested in developing a conceptual framework, or do you think that theory is largely irrelevant?

As fully as possible, explore your responses to these questions:

(?) What are the theoretical ideas or concepts that you refer to most often, in terms of your own personal thinking about counselling issues, and your discussions with other people around these matters? How deeply have you studied these concepts? Have you mainly learned about these ideas or concepts from general reading, or listening to other people, or is your knowledge based on extensive reading?

(?) What are the theoretical tensions or dilemmas that you are aware of in your work as a counsellor (or in your reading as a trainee/student)? Are there times when you are caught between different ways of making sense of a client (or any person you are helping), or of your role in relation to a client? What do you do when you have this kind of experience?

(?) What is the direction of your theoretical development? Are there earlier theoretical ideas that you have 'grown out of'? Where do you feel that your theoretical interests are heading? What do you feel you want to (or *need* to) read next?

(?) For you, what is the ideal balance between making sense of the process of counselling in terms of an explicit theoretical formulation, and arriving at an intuitive, gut response to what is happening?

(?) On the whole, how satisfied are you with your current relationship with counselling theory? Do you feel that you may sometimes over-theorize, and thus perhaps lose touch with what is taking place in the moment? Or do you struggle to detach yourself from the moment-by-moment complexity of counselling and perhaps lack an ability to develop a conceptual overview?

Some counsellors find great satisfaction in working within a well-defined set of theoretical constructs, which they continue to find meaningful throughout their career. Other counsellors see themselves as participating on an intellectual journey, always seeking to know more and understand more fully. Both positions are perfectly valid.

Similarly, there are approaches to counselling (such as person-centred) that take the view that factors such as the quality of the relationship between counsellor and client, and the depth of experiencing of issues, are much more important than theoretical analysis. Other approaches, such as Transactional Analysis or CBT, are based on the systematic application of theoretical concepts in case formulation. Again, both positions appear to be equally effective.

Developing a personal approach involves taking account of your own individual relationship with theory. Some of the key issues associated with the role of theory in counselling are discussed in Chapter 3 of *An Introduction to Counselling*.

Meta-theories – how do they shape the way you think about counselling?

Mainstream approaches to counselling – psychodynamic, person-centred and cognitive-behavioural – are based in competing psychological theories of personality. Making a choice between these alternative psychological models is no easy task. For the most part, the evidence from research does not make it possible to state with any confidence that one psychological model is correct or valid, and that another one is wrong. In practice, espousing a theoretical approach, or combination of approaches, tends to be influenced by other, broader sets of beliefs, values and ideas with which the counsellor identifies himself or herself. These ideas and beliefs can be described as *meta-theories*, because they can be viewed as over-arching systems of thought within which psychological theories are embedded. The aim of this exercise is to identify the meta-theories that are significant for you, and to explore the ways in which these ideas shape your approach to counselling.

Instructions

On a piece of paper, create a display of the ideas or systems of thought that are most significant in your life. Place the ideas that are most central for you in the middle of the page, and the ones that are less important near the edge. These ideas can be drawn from a variety of domains:

1. Religious and spiritual beliefs that are important for you – for example, Christianity, Buddhism, Islam, atheism;

2. Philosophical ideas that are meaningful for you – for example, existentialism, phenomenology, empiricism, rationalism, postmodernism, constructivism;

> An interdisciplinary perspective on counselling is discussed on pages 13–14 of *An Introduction to Counselling*.

3. Political ideologies that you support or oppose – for example socialism, capitalism, individualism, feminism, environmentalism, consumerism, trade unionism, gay rights;

4. Academic or scientific disciplines that have had a formative impact on the way you view the world – for example, mathematics, sociology, anthropology, economics, history;

5. Forms of artistic expression and creativity through which you find meaning – for example, poetry, drama, cinema, music.

Once you have drawn your personal 'meta-theory map', take some time to reflect on the implications of these ideas, beliefs and practices for your personal approach as a counsellor:

? Which sets of ideas are most relevant to your counselling theory and practice? Which ones are less relevant, or not at all relevant?

? In what ways might these ideas shape the way you are, and the choices you make as a counsellor?

? Which counselling theories and concepts are most compatible with your 'meta-theories'?

Further reading

Good sources of further reading around the psychology of personality, which explore the psychological models that underpin current therapeutic practice, are:

McAdams, D. (2000) *The Person: An Integrated Introduction*. New York: Wiley.

Monte, C. (1998) *Beneath the Mask: An Introduction to Theories of Personality*. New York: Wiley.

Pervin, L. (2000) *Personality: Theory and Research*. New York: Wiley.

Pervin, L. (2002) *Current Controversies and Issues in Personality*. New York: Wiley.

Some of the ways in which *meta-theories* can influence approaches to counselling are discussed in:

Howard, A. (2000) *Philosophy for Counselling and Psychotherapy: Pythagoras to Postmodernism*. London: Macmillan.

Thorne, B. and Dryden, W. (eds) (1993) *Counselling: Interdisciplinary Perspectives*. Buckingham: Open University Press.

Applying theory: making sense of personal experience

Earlier in the Workbook (Section 1) you were invited to write about a number of aspects of your own life that represented everyday therapeutic processes that you may have encountered either in the role of helper, or as someone seeking help from another person. A valuable means of developing an awareness of your preferred position in relation to theories of counselling and psychotherapy is to reflect on what you have written about yourself, in theoretical terms.

Learning tasks

1. Read through some of the autobiographical pieces that you have written, for example your *Story of a Helping Relationship, Early Memories*, or *Experience of Changing your Own Behaviour*. Identify any theoretical concepts that are embedded, or implicit, in what you have written. For example, you may have described your experience in terms of being *reinforced* by certain outcomes (a behavioural concept), or as involving the achievement of *insight* (a psychodynamic concept). Is there consistency in the constructs and terminology that you have used? If there is, what does this discovery suggest to you about your preferred theoretical position?

2. Imagine that you are a counsellor who is steeped in a specific theoretical orientation (for example, person-centred). To do this, you might wish to read the relevant chapter in *An Introduction to Counselling*, and other sources, and immerse yourself in that theoretical approach for a while. From this perspective, read and interpret a sample of the stories that you wrote in Section 1. Be rigorous in only applying ideas from that specific approach, and do your best to make use of a full range of concepts from the approach you have selected. Once you have done this, consider the following questions:

    ? How satisfactory has this theoretical perspective been in accounting for all aspects of your experience? In what ways did using this perspective lead you to focus on some areas of experience at the expense of others?

    ? In what ways, and to what extent, did the use of a specific framework enable you to develop a new or fresh understanding of the events and experiences you had written about?

    ? What were the practical implications that were generated by the theoretical framework you applied? Did the theory you were applying stimulate further thinking and planning about how you might address issues in your life that were problematic to you?

    ? Reflecting on the 'experiment' of imaging yourself into a theoretical stance – in general terms, how credible and convincing for you was the theoretical 'reading' or interpretation that you developed?

3. Apply different, alternative theoretical perspectives to your autobiographical writings, following the guidelines in the previous paragraph. Which of the perspectives seemed most useful to you? In what ways? Are there aspects of different theoretical models that you might wish to combine, to arrive at an ideal overall framework for understanding? If so, what are the principles or values that inform your choice?

4) Are there some concepts or perspectives that seem alien or wrong to you, which you just find impossible to apply? If there are, it may be helpful to consult someone who is comfortable with using these concepts. It may be valuable to develop an understanding of what does *not* work for you, in terms of theory, as a means of sharpening your appreciation of what *does* fit within your personal approach.

Empathy: a key concept in counselling

Rogers suggested that when the counsellor/helper is able to understand the client, and accurately convey that understanding, the person will become more able to accept previously denied or warded-off aspects of their own experience.

In person-centred counselling, it is important to stay within the 'frame of reference' of the client, to 'walk in their shoes', to 'see the world they way they see it', and not to respond on the basis of your own projections, experiences or to offer advice.

Read what Carl Rogers (1961) said about empathy:

> Various aspects of the concept of empathy are discussed on pages 99, 169–73, 215–6 and 319 of *An Introduction to Counselling*.

The state of empathy, or being empathic, is to perceive the internal frame of reference of another with accuracy and with the emotional components and meanings which pertain thereto as if one were the person, but without ever losing the 'as if' condition. Thus it means to sense the hurt or the pleasure of another as he senses it and to perceive the causes thereof as he perceives them, but without ever losing the recognition that it is 'as if' I were hurt or pleased and so forth. If this 'as if' quality is lost, then the state is one of identification. (p. 62)

and in 1975:

The way of being with another person which is termed empathic has several facets. It means entering the private perceptual world of the other and becoming thoroughly at home in it. It involves being sensitive, moment to moment, to the changing felt meanings which flow in this other person, to the fear or rage or tenderness or confusion or whatever that he/she is experiencing. It means temporarily living in his/her life, moving about in it delicately without making judgements, sensing meanings of which he/she is scarcely aware, but not trying to uncover feelings of which the person is totally unaware, since this would be too threatening. It includes communicating your sensings of his/her world as you look with fresh and unfrightened eyes at elements of which the individual is fearful. It means frequently checking with him/her as to the accuracy of your sensings, and being guided by the responses you receive. You are a confident companion to the person in his/her inner world. By pointing to the possible meanings in the flow of his/her experiencing you help the person to focus on this useful type of referent, to experience the feelings more fully, and to move forward in the experiencing.

To be with another person in this way means that for the time being you lay aside the views and values you hold for yourself in order to enter another's world without prejudice. In some sense it means that you lay aside your own self and this can only be done by a person who is secure enough in himself that he knows he will not get lost in what may turn out to be the strange or bizarre world of the other, and can comfortably return to his own world when he wishes. (Rogers, 1975: 2–10)

Consider the following questions:

 What are the key ideas in these statements? What are the changes in emphasis between the two?

 To what extent do Rogers's words capture what empathy means to you? You may find it helpful to refer back to what you wrote in response to the *Experience of feeling understood* in Section 2, and reflect on whether the description given by Rogers matches your own experience.

 What would you wish to add to Rogers's ideas, in order to arrive at an account of the process of empathy that fully captured your own sense of this phenomenon?

(?) What are the personal challenges raised for you by these descriptions of empathy? How readily can you 'sense the hurt or the pleasure of another' or 'lay aside the views and values you hold for yourself in order to enter another's world'. What helps or hinders you in achieving this kind of contact with others?

(?) How important is the concept of empathy for you, in terms of your own personal thinking about counselling? Is it an essential force for therapeutic change? Or is it merely one element of relationship building?

Making sense of *self*

A comparison between the ideas of *self* and *ego* can be found on pages 286–7 of *An Introduction to Counselling*.

The word 'self' is part of everyday language: 'I couldn't find anyone to help me lift the box so I did it myself'. *Self* is also a concept that occurs in most theories of therapy – for example self-concept (person-centred), self-object (Object Relations) and self-efficacy (CBT). The fact that everyday and 'technical' uses of the term co-exist mean that there is much opportunity for confusion. It is valuable to be clear about your own personal understanding of the idea of *self*.

Exploring your understanding of the idea of self

1. Reflect on the words you use when talking about counselling. How often do you use the term 'self'? How often do you use other terms that are broadly equivalent, such as 'ego', 'identity', or 'personality'? Which of these terms sits most comfortably with your way of seeing relationships?

2. How important is the idea of *self* for you? Some philosophical approaches, such as Buddhism and postmodernism, take the view that 'self' in an illusion. Some cultures make little use of the idea of an individual self, preferring to talk in terms of 'we'.

3. How do you define 'self'? In Section 1 of the Workbook, you may have completed an exercise titled *The self puzzle*, in which you drew a picture of your 'self', with each of the 'parts' of the self labelled. Look again at that picture, and consider which of the following elements of different self-theories are expressed within it:

   ⇒ *Core and peripheral self.* Is there a central section of your puzzle or map, which contains qualities or values that are, in some way, essential to your sense of who you are? Are there sections towards the edge of your page that describe values and qualities that are somehow less essential?

   ⇒ *Internalized self-objects.* Object Relations theory suggests that we include, within the self, images of significant others, or parts of these others (such as their words or voice) that are important to our emotional functioning. Are there any such figures in your puzzle?

   ⇒ *Relational self.* Have you portrayed a relational self (lots of links to other people) or a boundaried, autonomous self?

   ⇒ *Multiplicity or unity.* Does your picture convey a sense of a single entity, or are there separate parts (sub-selves) that are separated off from each other?

   ⇒ *Self-esteem and self-acceptance.* Person-centred theory assumes that the extent to which a person accepts or values all aspects of self is an indicator of well-being. To what extent is acceptance a theme in your picture?

   ⇒ *Self-efficacy.* Cognitive-behavioural theorists argue that the extent to which a person views him/herself as being in control, and able to bring about change, is a key dimension of self. Does efficacy, or agency, appear as a theme in your drawing?

   ⇒ *Other dimensions of self.* There are other dimensions of self that may be relevant to you: conscious-unconscious, actualization and fulfilment, spirituality.

Once you have explored your self puzzle in the light of these ideas, it may be useful to reflect on the implications of what you have found for your espoused theoretical model. To what extent is your own personal 'theory of self' consistent with your theoretical stance?

Further reading

Each of the main theoretical approaches to counselling, outlined in Chapters 4–11 of *An Introduction to Counselling*, has its own way of understanding the nature of the self. It may be worthwhile looking again at these chapters in the light of what you have learned through this exercise about your own personal theory of self.

How theory is applied in practice: key cases

Over the years a number of counsellors and psychotherapists (and some clients) have written case studies that express the complexity of their experiences of counselling. Some of these case histories have become highly influential within the field, because they have been regarded as defining how 'master therapists' carry out therapy.

It is very useful to read case studies, because they provide a unique insight into the ways that therapists think about their work. A case study also allows the reader to arrive at their own sense of whether the approach to thinking about and working with clients that is being described actually fits with their own personal way of being.

When you are reading or viewing a case study, keep in mind that it is a *representation* of therapy, which highlights some aspects of what is happening and glosses over other elements. You may find the following questions helpful in reflecting on a case:

(?)   How did you feel about the therapist? Would you have liked him/her to be your therapist? Why, or why not?

(?)   How did you feel about the client? If you had been the counsellor, how might you have tried to work with him/her?

(?)   What is helpful and/or unhelpful in what the therapist did?

(?)   To what extent does the effectiveness of the therapy rely on the application of specific techniques, as opposed to the creation of a strong relationship? What is the balance between 'specific' and 'non-specific' elements?

(?)   How strictly did the therapist keep to his or her espoused theoretical model? If and when he or she diverged from the model, was this useful or did it seem to be a mistake?

Further reading

Some sources for cases that have been widely influential within the field are:

Axline, V. (1971) *Dibs: In Search of Self*. London: Penguin. An account of the use of a client-centred or person-centred approach in therapy with a disturbed young boy.

Dryden, W. (ed.) (1986) *Key Cases in Psychotherapy*. London: Croom Helm.

Gay, P. (ed.) (1995) *The Freud Reader*. London: Vintage. Includes several classic cases, along with other important papers by Freud.

Wedding, D. and Corsini, R.J. (eds) (2000) *Case Studies in Psychotherapy*. Itasca, IL: FE Peacock.

Yalom, I. (1989) *Love's Executioner*. London: Penguin. A series of fictionalized case studies by Irving Yalom, one of the leading figures in existential therapy and a highly influential contemporary writer on therapy.

Applying cognitive-behavioural concepts

Cognitive-behavioural therapy (CBT) is one of the most widely used forms of psychological therapy currently in use. Even if you regard yourself as not a CBT therapist, it is important to be able to develop an appreciation of the way in which problems can be conceptualized and worked with from this perspective. The intellectual origins of CBT are in behavioural psychology. The reflective activities described below illustrate how two of the basic principles of behavioural psychology – operant and classical conditioning – can be applied in the analysis of everyday problems.

Operant or instrumental conditioning (functional analysis)

Choose an ordinary behaviour that you engage in every day. Examples might be: drinking tea, drinking coffee, drinking beer or wine, listening to the radio, dancing, reading the newspaper and so on.

Analyze this behaviour in behavioural terms:

1 What are the stimuli, situations or antecedents that elicit this behaviour?

2 What is the actual behaviour? Describe it in as much concrete detail as possible. Can you describe it in terms of a sequence of behaviours?

3 What are the consequences of the behaviour? What follows it? How is the behaviour reinforced or rewarded? Are there contingencies of reinforcement that cause the behaviour to occur more frequently, or less frequently?

It can be instructive to try this analysis out on a range of different behaviours, including 'habits' that you might consider to be problematic in your life, such as smoking, eating chocolate, nail-biting, procrastinating, and so on.

Classical conditioning

Choose *one* situation in which you feel moderately afraid, but which you feel okay about exploring in a brief exercise. Examples could include: speaking in a seminar group, meeting new people, being in an exam, being in a lift, looking out of a high window, touching a snake or spider.

The following prompts take you through an analysis of your behaviour in terms of the application of a classical conditioning model to the acquisition of a conditioned emotional response.

(?) What was the first time you remember feeling like this? What were the original unconditioned stimuli and responses (reflex responses) from which this fear pattern originated? It may be hard to recall such an incident, if you have had this fear for some time. You may need to imagine a hypothetical situation in which you first experienced this fear.

(?) What was the process of *generalization* that resulted in the present pattern of fearfulness?

The main concepts of behavioural psychology, and a discussion of how they have been applied in therapy, are covered on pages 123–31 of *An Introduction to Counselling*.

(?) In what ways has this fear led to an *avoidance* of certain situations or stimuli?

(?) To what extent has this avoidance resulted in the perpetuation or *maintenance* of the fear pattern?

(?) Applying a behavioural approach, what could you do to *extinguish* the connection between certain situations, and a fear response, that you have identified in this analysis?

Again, it can be interesting to try this analysis out on different behaviours.

Reflect on what you have learned from engaging with these exercises in terms of your relationship with CBT as a way of making sense of personal problems:

(?) How useful did you find the application of these basic CBT concepts?

(?) Can these ways of thinking about problems be integrated or reconciled with other theoretical frameworks you espouse (e.g. psychodynamic, person-centred) or do they imply a completely different understanding of persons and lives?

Irrational beliefs and dysfunctional self-talk

Although contemporary cognitive-behavioural therapy (CBT) is ultimately derived from the behavioural learning theories of Skinner and Pavlov, the emphasis in recent years has been on applying these principles to analysing and changing cognitive processes and content – the way that a person thinks about his or her problems. This learning activity invites you to explore some of the ways in which your own behaviour is influenced by such cognitive processes.

Identify *one* situation or recurring scenario that you find difficult to cope with. Examples might include such everyday situations as saying no to a request that someone has made of you, lacking confidence when working on a task, or feeling anxious, tense and afraid. Your task is to consider how you might apply the ideas of Ellis regarding irrational beliefs, and of Meichenbaum concerning dysfunctional thinking/self-talk, to develop a better understanding of this problem.

1   *Step 1.* Describe the situation or scenario in as much detail as possible. What triggers the event? What do you do, in terms of specific actions and behaviours? Most important, what goes through your head at these moments – what are you thinking? What do you pay attention to?

2   *Step 2.* Can you identify *irrational beliefs* that may be triggered by the situation? Irrational beliefs are exaggerated ways of thinking about yourself. An example might be 'I must be perfect and do everything faultlessly ... otherwise I am a completely useless person'.

3   *Step 3.* Can you identify any sequences of *self-talk* that accompany your behaviour? What is your 'stream of consciousness'? Is there some kind of voice in your head that could be making statements such as 'you'll never get this right' or 'no one will believe you could have the right answer'?

4   *Step 4.* To what extent, and in what ways, do these irrational or self-defeating beliefs and cognitions undermine your ability to cope more positively with the situation you are exploring?

> The use of cognitive analysis in CBT is discussed on pages 132–8 of *An Introduction to Counselling.*

(Note: it can be hard to recall dysfunctional cognitive processes after the event. You may find it useful to carry around a notebook for a few days, and write down irrational beliefs and critical self-talk at the time they occur.)

Once you have completed this analysis, you may find it helpful to consider how CBT methods might be used to help you to change these patterns of thinking. For example: how might the situation you have described be re-framed, how might sequences of self-criticism be interrupted, how might irrational beliefs be challenged?

Finally, reflect on what you have learned from this activity in relation to your theoretical approach to counselling:

?   How useful did you find the application of these CBT concepts?

?   Can these ways of analysing a problem be integrated or reconciled with other theoretical frameworks you espouse (e.g. psychodynamic, person-centred) or do they imply a completely different understanding of persons and lives?

What difference would it make to apply this kind of analysis with the help of another person? What impact might the quality of the therapeutic relationship have on the benefit you might gain from using this technique?

Developing a cognitive-behavioural case formulation

The aim of this learning task is to give you some experience of what it is like to apply cognitive-behavioural methods in practice.

CBT interventions are reviewed on pages 138–9 of *An Introduction to Counselling*.

First, you need to identify a problem in your own life that is real but limited (i.e. not too upsetting to look at). This could be something like smoking, eating too much choco-late, nail-biting, feeling anxious making a presentation to a group, avoiding completing a piece of work, and so on. Do not choose an issue that is too personal, difficult, upsetting or traumatic. Choose a problem that is meaningful, yet manageable in the context of a learning exercise: it is not helpful to open up difficulties or feelings that may spill over from the exercise and be disruptive to your life.

Your task is to formulate a cognitive-behavioural programme to deal with this problem.

Follow these steps:

1. Build up a full description of the thoughts and actions/behaviours that make up the problem. Describe in detail the sequence of stimuli, responses and reinforcers that maintain the 'problem' in place. You may find it helpful to 'map' you analysis of the problem behaviour on a large sheet of paper.

2. Identify your optimal scenario or goal – what is your target for change? How would you – ideally – like to behave in relation to this area of your life?

3. Develop a list of possible techniques or interventions that might be employed to help you to move towards your goal. Work out which order you might try these interventions – where would you start?

Once you have completed your 'case formulation' along the lines described above, consider the following questions:

? How helpful do you think this approach would be in overcoming the problem? What other approach to counselling might help you better? Why?

? Have you tried any of these strategies before? Did they help? If not, then why didn't they help?

Further reading

Good sources for further learning about the use of case formulation are:

Bruch, M. and Bond, F.W. (1998) *Beyond Diagnosis: Case Formulation Approach in CBT*. Chichester: Wiley.

Eells, T.D. (ed.) (1997) *Handbook of Psychotherapy Case Formulation*. New York: Guilford Press.

Congruence and authenticity: conceptualizing the use of self in counselling

Within the person-centred approach, the capacity of the counsellor to make constructive use of their own feelings, reactions and imaginings in relation to the client is considered as one of the key aspects of effective therapy (Lietaer, 1993). This counsellor's 'use of self' is generally referred to within the person-centred approach as *congruence*. However, within the wider humanistic psychology framework of which the person-centred approach is a part, many other concepts have been employed: authenticity, transparency, genuineness, openness, presence, honesty, resonance. In psychodynamic theory, similar processes are discussed in terms of *counter-transference*. Any counsellor needs to work out his or her position on this aspect of their relationship with clients: how central is it? How can it be encouraged? What are its limits?

> These issues are examined in *An Introduction to Counselling* on pages 174–7 and 300–2.

The 'use of self' also involves the idea of 'self-disclosure' – telling the client about yourself. The concept of self-disclosure has been used to encompass both *immediacy* in the therapy situation (i.e. feeding back to the client your immediate reaction to what he or she has said) and also the sharing of autobiographical information. It is probably most sensible to retain 'self-disclosure' for the latter set of activities – sharing autobiographical information.

Learning tasks

1) Reflect on the words that you prefer to talk about your own 'use of self' in counselling. What are the implications of using certain concepts rather than others? Specifically, what are for you the similarities and differences between the ideas of 'congruence', 'counter-transference' and 'self-disclosure'? Are there other words (authenticity, honesty, genuinenenss, presence) that seem to have a better 'fit' with your personal experience?

2) Different facets of the person-centred idea of congruence are expressed in the following definitions:

Congruence is the state of being of the counsellor when her outward responses to the client consistently match her inner feelings and sensations she has in relation to the client. (Mearns and Thorne, 1999: 75)

... the feelings the therapist is experiencing are available to him, and to his awareness, and he is able to live these feelings, be them, and to communicate them if appropriate. No one fully achieves this condition, yet the more the therapist is able to listen acceptantly to what is going on within himself, and the more he is able to be the complexity of his feelings, without fear, the higher the degree of his congruence. (Rogers, 1961: 61)

At every moment there occur a great many feelings and events in the therapist. Most of these concern the client and the present moment. The therapist need not wait passively till the client expresses something intimate or therapeutically relevant. Instead, he can draw upon his own momentary experiencing and find there an ever present reservoir from which he can draw, and with which he can initiate, deepen and carry on therapeutic interaction even with an unmotivated, silent or externalised person ... To respond truly from within me I must, of course, pay some attention to what is going on within me ... I require a few steps of *self-attention*, a few moments in which I attend to what I feel. (Gendlin, 1967: 120–1)

Stay with these definitions for a few moments. Reflect on them and consider the implications they might hold for you. For example:

(?) How able are you to 'listen acceptantly' to yourself? To what extent do you have enough basic self-acceptance to allow yourself to do this? Under what circumstances do you tend to doubt yourself?

(?) What do you do with your *fear* in a counselling situation? Can you allow yourself to remain afraid, or even to move in the direction of danger?

(?) Do you allow yourself to draw on your 'momentary experiencing'? Have you developed the skill of taking a few steps of 'self-attention' now and again?

Once you have explored these tasks, reflect on the significance of this topic for you as a counsellor: where does congruence (or whatever other term you would use) sit within your personal approach?

Further reading

Books which may facilitate extended exploration of this important topic are:

Rowan, J. and Jacobs, M. (2002) *The Therapist's Use of Self*. Buckingham: Open University Press.

Wosket, V. (1999) *The Therapeutic Use of Self: Counselling Practice, Research and Supervision*. London: Routledge.

Experiencing authenticity

Congruence and authenticity are discussed in *An Introduction to Counselling* on pages 174–7 and 300–2.

It is a mistake to regard authenticity or congruence as merely a matter of values or philosophy, for example as a therapeutic concept derived from an existential view that 'good faith' is a necessary quality in life. It is similarly a mistake to view it as just a matter of style: this is the way that humanistic therapists want to present themselves to the world. For person-centred and humanistic counsellors, authenticity is central to practice. These learning tasks offer opportunities to reflect on your personal experience of offering, and receiving, authentic contact.

Learning Task 1. Mearns and Thorne (1999) provide a list of concrete ways in which a personal response to a client may be expressed. They formulate these ways as a set of questions that a therapist might ask about his or her willingness to be involved in the relationship with a client:

Can I dare to:

- Feel the feelings that are within me?
- Hold my client when I feel he needs to be held?
- Show my anger when that is strongly felt?
- Admit my distraction when challenged about it?
- Voice my irritation when that grows?
- Put words to my affection when that is there?
- Shout when something is seething inside me?
- Be spontaneous even when I don't know where that will lead?
- Be forceful as well as gentle?
- Be gentle as well as forceful?
- Use my sensuous self in relation to my client?
- Step out from behind my 'professional façade'?
- Can I dare to be *me* in response to my client?

How do you respond to these questions, either in terms of your own experience as a counsellor, or (if you have yet to begin working with clients), how you anticipate you might feel in relation to clients?

Learning Task 2. In your own personal experience (either in therapy or elsewhere) how often have you felt that another person has been really congruent or genuine with you? Think of times when this has happened. Take a specific instance: what impact did the experience have on you? How did it effect your relationship with that person?

Learning Task 3. When are you 'open to your self'? What are the circumstances under which you make discoveries about yourself, or deepen your story of who you are?

Reflecting on these tasks

What have you learned about yourself, and your approach to counselling, from engaging with these tasks? How do you understand the *impact* of authentic contact, as part of a therapeutic process? You may find it useful to compare your thoughts on this issue with the list of impacts provided on page 175 of *An Introduction to Counselling*.

Further reading

Learning Task 3 is adapted from Mearns, D. and Thorne, B. (2000) *Person-centred Therapy Today: New Frontiers in Theory and Practice.* London: Sage.

How important is the balance between problems and solutions?

Over the last decade, there has been a powerful movement within counselling and psychotherapy away from a preoccupation with helping people to analyse their *problems*, and towards the goal of building up the person's strengths and skills, and helping them to find practical *solutions*.

> An outline of solution-focused therapy can be found on pages 146–52 of *An Introduction to Counselling.*

This trend is reflected in various approaches to counselling, ranging from the emphasis on personal growth that is found in humanistic therapies, to the goal-oriented nature of behaviour therapy. However, it has found its clearest expression in the *solution-focused therapy* developed by Imsoo Kim Berg, Steven de Shazer and Bill O'Hanlan.

This learning task gives you an opportunity to reflect on some of the implications of the solution-focused approach.

Think about situations where you have been involved in a counselling relationship, trying to help another person. Think also about occasions when you have been the recipient of such help.

In these situations:

(?) How necessary was it for you (or the person you were helping) to talk about the detail of their problems?

(?) How helpful was it to talk about solutions (strengths, 'good news', achievements)?

(?) What is your sense of the right balance between a problem focus and a solution focus in the counselling episode(s) you have been looking at?

(?) What has made the difference for you, at times when you have struggled with an area of difficulty in your life: understanding the origins of these problems, or finding ways of changing how you cope?

More broadly:

(?) What does a person gain by becoming aware of, and taking note of, their solutions to problems?

(?) What can a person learn, or gain, from becoming aware of the possible causes of their problems?

In considering these questions, what have you learned about your own position as a counsellor, in relation to the adoption of a solution-focused, or problem-oriented approach to working with clients?

Specific techniques or common factors

Over the last 50 years there has been a great deal of research which has compared the effectiveness of different models of therapy. This research has arrived at an apparently paradoxical conclusion: all approaches to therapy, no matter what their methods, appear to yield equivalent results in terms of client outcomes. These findings have stimulated debate over the role of common, or non-specific factors in counselling and psychotherapy.

A common factor is a therapeutic process which occurs in any kind of therapy. A specific technique, by contrast, is an intervention that forms part of a particular named approach to therapy.

> The common factors perspective is discussed on pages 55–61 of *An Introduction to Counselling*.

Consider the list of common and non-specific factors presented in Table 1, and then respond to the questions which follow.

Table 1

Common factors	Specific techniques
Encouraging the client to have positive expectations for change	Systematic desensitization (behaviour therapy)
The therapist being warmly and genuinely interested in the client	Interpretation of dreams (psychoanalysis)
Offering a safe environment within which to talk about shameful or difficult attitudes and experiences	Two-chair dialogues (Gestalt Therapy) Empathic reflection of meaning (person-centred approach)
The counsellor having the status of a socially sanctioned, credible, 'healer'	Counsellor congruence (person-centred) or use of counter-transference (psychodynamic)
Having permission to express emotion	
Being offered a framework for understanding one's problems	Writing a 're-authoring' letter to the client (narrative therapy)
Being introduced to a set of procedures or rituals which will bring about change	Challenging irrational beliefs and destructive self-talk (CBT)
Observing at close hand a person (the counsellor) who is skilful in dealing with relationships	Exploring the assumptions that inform one's worldview (philosophical counselling)

Key questions for reflection

(?) To what extent can the therapeutic impact of each of these specific techniques be explained or understood in terms of the list of common factors in the left-hand column?

(?) Are there any therapeutic processes associated with the specific techniques in the right-hand column that *cannot* be reduced to common factors? How would you describe or characterize these 'uncommon' factors?

(?) What is your own personal position on the relationship between specific techniques and common factors?

Positioning your practice in relation to social and political factors

Counselling and psychotherapy have evolved as forms of help that typically operate at an *individual* level. One of the most powerful critiques of contemporary counselling comes from those who argue that it functions within society to promote an over-individualized approach to problems that are in fact cultural, social and political in nature. This critique has lead in two directions:

⟹   An argument that counselling should be replaced by some form of social and political activism;

⟹   Attempts to make counselling more socially informed.

These issues are touched on throughout *An Introduction to Counselling*, and are discussed in depth in Chapter 14.

In your portfolio, you might like to write about where you have arrived in relation to these questions:

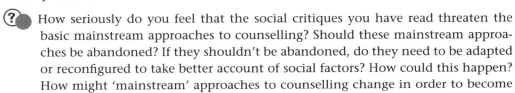   How seriously do you feel that the social critiques you have read threaten the basic mainstream approaches to counselling? Should these mainstream approaches be abandoned? If they shouldn't be abandoned, do they need to be adapted or reconfigured to take better account of social factors? How could this happen? How might 'mainstream' approaches to counselling change in order to become more socially inclusive?

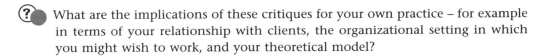   What are the implications of these critiques for your own practice – for example in terms of your relationship with clients, the organizational setting in which you might wish to work, and your theoretical model?

Further reading

A stimulating collection of papers on the issues around the social role of counselling can be found in:

House, R. and Totton, N. (eds) (1998) *Implausible Professions: Arguments for Pluralism and Autonomy in Psychotherapy and Counselling*. Ross-on-Wye: PCCS Books.

The idea of the unconscious

It is part of everyday common-sense to admit that there are times when one is not consciously aware of what one is doing, or why a particular action has been taken. However, the notion of *the unconscious*, as used in psychoanalytic and psychodynamic approaches to counselling and psychotherapy, goes far beyond this common-sense view, in assuming that the unconscious mind operates in a highly specific manner. Take some time to read carefully, and reflect on, the following key passage, written by Freud towards the end of his career:

… what is meant by 'conscious', we need not discuss; it is beyond all doubt … we call 'unconscious' any mental process the existence of which we are obliged to assume … but of which we are not directly aware … we call a process 'unconscious' when we have to assume that it was active *at a certain time*, although *at that time* we knew nothing about it … Psycho-analysis has impressed us very strongly with the new idea that large and important regions of the mind are normally removed from the knowledge of the ego, so that the processes that occur in them must be recognised as unconscious in the true dynamic sense of the term … The *id* is the obscure inaccessible part of our personality … a chaos, a cauldron of seething excitement. We suppose that it is somewhere in direct contact with somatic processes, and takes over from them instinctual needs and gives them mental expression, but we cannot say in what substratum this contact is made. These instincts fill it with energy, but it has no organisation and no unified will, only an impulse to obtain satisfaction for the instinctual needs, in accordance with the pleasure-principle. The laws of logic – above all, the law of contradiction – do not hold for processes in the id. Contradictory impulses exist side by side without neutralising each other or drawing apart … There is nothing in the *id* which can be compared to negation, and we are astonished to find in it an exception to the philosophers' assertion that space and time are necessary forms of our mental acts. In the *id* there is nothing corresponding to the idea of time, no recognition of the passage of time … no alteration of mental processes by the passage of time … impulses which have never got beyond the *id*, and even impressions which have been pushed down into the *id* by repression, are virtually immortal and are preserved for whole decades as though they had only recently occurred. They can only be recognised as belonging to the past, deprived of their significance, and robbed of their charge of energy, after they have been made conscious by the work of analysis, and no small part of the therapeutic effect of analytic treatment rests upon this fact … Naturally, the *id* knows no values, no good and evil, no morality … (Freud, 1933: 93–100)

Is this a definition of 'the unconscious' with which you agree? Does it fully capture the way that you might wish to use this concept in your counselling work? If it does not reflect the way you view 'the unconscious', then what kind of alternative definition might you suggest? Or is it possible to imagine conducting therapy without making any reference to unconscious processes?

Further reading

These issues are explored further in Edwards, D. and Jacobs, M. (2003) *Conscious and Unconscious*. Buckingham: Open University Press.

What brings about change? The relative importance of cognition and emotion

All theories of therapy acknowledge that the process of change involves an interplay of *cognitive* factors (changing the way that the person thinks about an issue) and *emotion* (for example, expressing repressed feelings). However, theoretical approaches differ significantly in the extent to which they emphasize one or the other of these key factors. For instance, the cognitive therapies of Beck and Ellis regard cognition as primary, with emotions being determined by the way that a person perceives or construes events. By contrast, both psychoanalysis and person-centred counselling regard the inner emotional life, or 'felt sense' of the person as the main driver of therapeutic change, and would view changes in the way a person thinks about an issue as following from changes in they way they feel.

What is your own position in relation to the relative importance of emotion and cognition? Your own personal experience and belief in relation to this issue will inevitably shape your choice of theoretical orientation.

Learning task

Read through the descriptions of personal learning and change that you created in response to some of the learning tasks in Section 2 of this Workbook. Are there any recurrent themes in these descriptions concerning the relative importance of emotion and cognition? Do your descriptions include mainly examples of cognitive *insight* and *understanding*, or have you mainly written about moments of emotional release and catharsis?

When reflecting on what this learning activity has produced for you, it may be helpful to consider the following questions:

(?) What have you learned about the relative importance of cognitive and emotional processes in your own way of understanding change in therapy?

(?) How well does your own 'take' on cognition and emotion correspond to the theoretical approaches that interest you, or with which you have identified yourself?

(?) What is your own personal model of the links between cognition and emotion? In your opinion, how do they link up – what causes what?

(?) How long have you held these ideas about cognition and emotion? Where and how did you learn them?

(?) What are the implications of your position of emotion-cognition for your *practice* as a counsellor?

Behind the theory: the life of the theorist

Theories of counselling and psychotherapy have tended to be associated with the ideas of 'key figures', such as Sigmund Freud or Carl Rogers. These leading theorists are often revered as brilliant thinkers who transformed the field through their genius. However, it is possible to view the importance of these individuals in a different light. Any theory of therapy can be regarded as a set of ideas and assumptions that reflect the cultural milieu within which they were generated. In important ways, the theories of Freud and Rogers became influential because they somehow reflected and articulated aspects of human experience that were challenging and significant in pre-World War I Europe (for Freud) and in post-World War II USA (for Rogers). The popularity of a theorist can be taken as indicating the extent to which his or her writings can operate as a channel for expressing the distinctive personal and interpersonal issues being faced by a particular group of people at a specific time in history. It is often pointed out that the childhood experiences of theorists such as Freud and Rogers play a large part in shaping their ideas. But, in important ways, these childhood experiences themselves may reflect broader aspects of the culture within which the person grew up.

In becoming a counsellor, it is essential to develop a theoretical framework with which client issues, and the process of therapy, can be understood. Inevitably, this theoretical framework will largely draw upon the ideas of a small number of writers and theorists. In order to gain a full appreciation of these theories, it can be very useful to learn about the lives of the theoreticians themselves. To a large extent, their theories evolved to enable them to make sense of issues within their own lives, and in the lives of people they knew.

A useful learning activity is to make an effort to go beyond the kind of brief biographical snapshot that is provided in books such as *An Introduction to Counselling* and other textbooks, and read actual biographies of theorists who have had an influence on you. Although autobiographical writing may also be interesting and relevant, it is likely to be grounded in the worldview of the author – a good biographer should have the capacity to place the life and work of his or her subject in a wider cultural context.

Further reading

Some biographies of therapy theorists that have been particularly well received include:

Cohen, D. (1997) *Carl Rogers. A Critical Biography*. London: Constable.

Gay, P. (1988) *Freud: A Life for our Time*. London: Dent.

Kirschenbaum, H. (1979) *On Becoming Carl Rogers*. New York: Dell.

Shepard, M. (1975) *Fritz*. New York: Bantam Books. (Biography of Fritz Perls)

A classic book, which explores the personal and cultural influences on a number of important therapy theorists, is:

Atwood, G. and Stolorow, R. (1993) *Faces in a Cloud: Intersubjectivity in Personality Theory*. Northvale, NJ: Jason Aronson.

The cultural context of understanding

How does your cultural identity influence your choice of counselling approach, in relation to training and practice? The impact of the social, cultural and family environment on the ideas of mainstream therapy theorists has been widely documented and discussed (see, for example, Atwood and Stolorow, 1993). But what are the ways in which *your own* social, cultural and family environment has shaped your personal approach to counselling?

In the *Exploring cultural identity* activity which was introduced earlier in this Workbook, you were invited to examine various aspects of your cultural origins and experiences. Looking back at what you wrote in response to that activity, consider the following questions:

? What are some of the values and beliefs that you associate with your cultural background, which seem most relevant to counselling?

? Imagine explaining your work as a counsellor, and the theories that you follow, to your grandmother. Would she be interested? Would she think that what you were doing was useful/what advice might she give you?

? Are there areas of tensions in your cultural identity? For example, your mother and father may have grown up in quite different cultures. Or there may have been times in your life when you have deliberately attempted to distance yourself from your culture of origin? How has your awareness of these tensions informed your understanding of counselling?

? Are there any rituals within your 'home' culture that could be viewed as having a psychotherapeutic function (for example, confessionals in church, family meetings, pilgrimages)? How might your engagement in such activities have informed your thinking about counselling?

? For you, is counselling a means of reinforcing and supporting the core values of your culture, or has it been a way of creating a new and different identity for yourself?

The underlying issue here is linked to the view of Lomas (1999: 25) that a person learning to become a counsellor needs to explore how best they can go about 'finding their own way, using their own intuition, learning to be themselves in the presence of someone who is asking for help'. Does you theoretical framework express who *you* are, including your sense of your own cultural identity?

What kind of therapeutic relationship?

Counselling is fundamentally a relationship between two persons. There is a wealth of evidence, from carefully conducted research studies and practical experience, that the quality of the therapeutic relationship has a huge impact on the amount that the client can gain from therapy.

However, relationships are difficult. We can all experience problems in making, keeping and ending relationships. The challenge, in becoming a counsellor, of seeking to be some kind of 'relationship expert', is considerable. Clients may be seeking all sorts of different kinds of relationships with their counsellor, and may create different kinds of barriers to forming a productive working 'alliance'. In turn, the needs and relationship patterns of the client may uncover gaps in the counsellor's capacity to relate.

These activities are intended to enable exploration of the relationship issues and challenges associated with counselling practice:

> These learning tasks complement Chapter 12 (The counselling relationship) of *An Introduction to Counselling*.

1. An experienced therapist, interviewed by Skovholt and Jennings (2004: 64), descri-bed his way of seeing the relationship between counsellor and client in the following terms:

One of the metaphors I often use with my clients is the metaphor of the 'Wilderness Guide', and the way I put that is they can hire me as a guide, because I know a lot about survival in the wilderness – my own, and I've travelled through a lot of wildernesses. I've got a compass, I can start a fire in the rain. I know how to make it through, but this is a new wilderness to me. I haven't been in this particular wilderness before, and so I can't quite predict what we're going to encounter.

In *An Introduction to Counselling*, pages 298–304, other metaphors of relationship found in mainstream approaches to counselling are discussed:

– Therapist as container;

– Therapist as authentic presence;

– Therapist as teacher, coach or scientist;

– The 'not-knowing' stance: therapist as editor.

Which of these images seem closest to the way that you experience yourself as being, or would aim to be, when in the role of counsellor? What are the implications of each of these metaphors, both for you and for the client?

2. Petruska Clarkson (1994: 42) argues that effective counsellors should be able to relate to clients, if necessary, at a transpersonal level:

the transpersonal relationship is … characterised … by a kind of intimacy and by an 'emptying of the ego' at the same time. It is rather as if the ego of even the personal unconscious of the psychotherapist is 'emptied out' of the therapeutic space, leaving space for something numinous to be created in the 'between' of the relationship … It implies a letting-go of skills, of knowledge, of experience, of preconceptions, even of the desire to heal, to be present. It is essentially allowing 'passivity' and receptiveness for which preparation is always inadequate. … It cannot be made to happen, it can only be encouraged in the same way that the inspirational muse of creativity cannot be forced, but needs to have the ground prepared or seized in the serendipitous moment of readiness.

To what extent is this form of therapeutic relationship meaningful for you? If it seems to you to represent an important dimension of counselling, how might you integrate this kind of possibility into your theoretical framework?

3. Return to the *Mapping your relationship patterns* exercise in an earlier Section of the Workbook. What did you write in response to that set of tasks? Looking now at what you wrote, what are the implications for your preferred ways of relating to clients? What are the implications in terms of difficulties that you might experience in relating fully to clients?

4. A wonderful book by Deborah Lott (1999: 1–2) provides a rich account of women's experiences of their relationships with their therapists. The idea for this book arose from her involvement with a group of women friends who met regularly to 'share their therapy war stories':

…it struck me that our exchanges resembled nothing so much as accounts of love affairs. We felt the same urgent need to get every detail straight, every word right …. We found the very structure of the therapeutic relationship problematic. It was inherently unequal: We needed our therapists more than they needed us, they were much more important to us than we were to them … To what extent was this even a *real* relationship, and if it wasn't real, *what* exactly was it? It wasn't friendship, and yet it was different from any other professional relationship we had ever had.

Is this an account of the therapeutic relation that you recognize? If it is, what significance does this perspective have for you, in terms of your personal approach?

In reflecting on these activities, it may be helpful to address the following questions:

(?) What is your image, or model, of the client-counsellor relationship?

(?) Which theories or concepts do you find useful in making sense of the therapeutic relationship?

(?) Are there aspects of the therapeutic relationship that, for you, seem to sit outside the established theories?

(?) How would you want a counsellor to be with you?

(?) How do you want to be with clients?

Dialogue between theorists

In the process of building a theoretical framework through which you can make sense of your work as a counsellor, you will almost certainly discover that you are drawn towards sets of ideas that are different, from competing traditions, or hard to integrate or reconcile with each other. It is perhaps easy to believe that, when this happens, it is an indicator of confusion, or a lack of ability either to integrate different perspectives or to be clear about where they overlap and where they diverge.

It may be more productive to regard such experiences as opportunities for learning. If you find meaning in different theories, then they are (by definition) meaningful for you. What may be lacking is a conceptual 'bridge' or idea that might enable you to see how the apparently conflicting ideas may be connected. This worksheet provides a technique that you might like to use to make such connections.

Dialogue between theorists

Choose two theorists whose work is important to you, but who seem to be saying quite different things (it is possible to carry out this exercise with more than two theorists, but it gets more complicated). Imagine that these theorists are in a room talking together, or are in email contact with each other. They are being stimulated and interviewed (by you) to engage in an exchange of views over some of their ideas. Write down this dialogue. Allow the dialogue to flow – the intention is not to come up with a version of each therapist's model that is necessarily factually accurate, but to begin to explore what their ideas mean *to you*.

For example, you may be convinced by Carl Rogers's ideas about the therapeutic 'core conditions', and also interested in Erik Erikson's model of stages of psychosocial development, but be at a loss to understand how they might fit together. Your imaginary dialogue might look something like:

Interviewer: One of you has a very clearly worked out theory of development, but the other – Rogers – seems to talk only about 'conditions of worth'. How can these perspectives be reconciled?

Carl Rogers: I always knew about Erik's ideas, but I didn't want to go down that road. My fear was always that a too definite model of development would detract from the client's 'frame of reference' and impose a set of assumptions based on the therapist's theory, rather than the client's reality.

Erik Erikson: I share that fear. That's why I always argued that these themes (identity, trust and so on) were in a sense always present – even if they seemed to be most prominent at certain ages. I always thought there were big connections to be made between autonomy, initiative, trust and so on, and the way you talked about empathy.

Carl Rogers: Yes, in a sense accurate empathy involves trust, and being separate, and having a good sense of your own identity.

This is only a hypothetical example. Your own dialogue might take a very different direction. Your protagonists may find they have a lot in common . . . or they may end up shouting at each other!

When you read through the dialogue you have created, look for the connections that have been made, and also for the new concepts that may act as 'bridges' between the two sets of ideas.

Are you postmodern?

According to many philosophers and social theorists, the closing years of the twentieth century saw the beginnings of a shift in the pattern of the dominant culture within Western industrial societies. The period from the 1700s to the mid-1900s can be viewed, historically, as comprising an era characterized by the growth and consolidation of a *modern* world, in which rationality, science, individualism, consumerism and the idea of progress were central to the way that people made sense of the world that they lived in. Psychology, and then counselling and psychotherapy, have been integral to the efforts of individuals to adapt to the demands of living in a modern society. Theories of therapy, and the research which has backed them up, have for the most part been formulated in accordance with the principles of modernity.

More recently, the ideas and social structures associated with modernity have started to fragment, and to be replaced by a different form of understanding. This new perspective has been described as *postmodernity*.

Some of the distinctive themes of postmodern thought have been described by Steiner Kvale (1992: 32–7) as:

… a loss of belief in an objective world and an incredulity towards meta-narratives of legitimation … with the collapse of universal meta-narratives, local narratives come into prominence. The particular, heterogeneous and changing language games replace the global horizon of meaning. With a pervasive decentralization, communal interaction and local knowledge become important in their own right … a postmodern world is characterized by a continual change of perspectives, with no underlying frame of reference, but rather a manifold of changing horizons … language and knowledge do not copy reality. Rather, language constitutes reality, each language constituting specific aspects of reality in its own way …. Postmodern though focuses on the *surface* …

> The significance of postmodern thinking for counselling and psychotherapy is discussed on pages 72–3 and 283–4 of *An Introduction to Counselling*.

A postmodern perspective is suspicious of all-encompassing 'grand theories', such as psychoanalysis and person-centred theory, and of any attempt to claim 'depth', in the sense of an underlying fundamental truth. Instead, postmodern thinking is interested in the way that realities are constructed through language.

To what extent do these ideas have meaning for you? If you are personally drawn to postmodern thinking, what are the implications for your approach as a counsellor? If you are not, what are the implications for your work with any client who does embrace these ideas?

Further reading

The relevance of postmodern philosophy for therapy practice is explored in:

Loewenthal, D. and Snell, R. (2003) *Post-modernism for Psychotherapists: A Critical Reader*. London: Brunner-Routledge.

Polkinghorne, D.E. (1992) Postmodern epistemology of practice, in S. Kvale (ed.) *Psychology and Postmodernism*. London: Sage.

Letter to a theorist

One of the techniques that is used in both personal journal writing, and in some forms of narrative therapy, is to compose a letter to a person with whom one would like to have a discussion, but who is not actually available to talk with. In bereavement work, for example, a person may write a letter to the person who has died. The value of an unsent letter is that it can provide an opportunity to get thoughts and feelings out into the open, and to begin, through a process of writing, to bring some order and structure to them.

This exercise invites you to make us of this technique to advance your understanding of theoretical issues in counselling.

Learning activity

Write a letter to a theorist who has some significance for you in terms of the way you make sense of counselling. Give yourself permission to write anything you wish to the person – what you like or do not like about his or her ideas, aspects of their thinking that make you angry or frustrated, questions that you have, counter-arguments, requests for help, compliments, invitations as so on.

It may be useful to consider different occasions that might call for such a letter:

➡ A theorist that you have just come across

➡ A theorist who is a major influence on your thinking

➡ A 'goodbye' letter to a theorist whose influence on your thinking you are trying to reduce or eliminate.

Once you have written the letter, reflect on what you have learned about yourself, and your theoretical stance as a counsellor.

The concept of transference

The concept of *transference* represents one of the key ideas within contemporary counselling and psychotherapy. Most counsellors and psychotherapists will acknowledge that clients may express strong feelings – both positive and negative – towards them. The *existence* of powerful and persistent client reactions to therapists is not disputed. However, there are major disagreements over the meaning and significance of such emotional responses. From a psychoanalytic or psychodynamic perspective, these reactions are indicators of patterns of early experience. From a person-centred or humanistic perspective, by contrast, these responses are understandable in terms of the here-and-now relationship between client and counsellor, often arising from the efforts of the counsellor to understand the client. These opposing positions are captured in the following passages, from Sigmund Freud (1938), and from a leading person-centred theorist and researcher, John Shlien (1984):

> The concept of transference is discussed in *An Introduction to Counselling* on pages 298–300

The patient is not satisfied with regarding the analyst in the light of reality as a helper and adviser who, moreover, is remunerated for the trouble he takes and who would himself be content with some such role as that of a guide on a difficult mountain climb. On the contrary, the patient sees in him the return, the reincarnation, of some important figure out of his childhood or past, and consequently transfers on to him feelings and reactions which undoubtedly applied to this prototype. This fact of transference soon proves to be a factor of undreamt-of importance, on the one hand an instrument of irreplaceable value and on the other hand a source of serious dangers. This transference is ambivalent: it comprises positive (affectionate) as well as negative (hostile) attitudes towards the analyst, who as a rule is put in the place of one or other of the patient's parents, his father or mother. So long as it is positive it serves us admirably. It alters the whole analytic situation; it pushes to one side the patient's rational aim of becoming healthy and free from his ailments. Instead of it there emerges the aim of pleasing the analyst and of winning his applause and love. It becomes the true motive force of the patient's collaboration; his weak ego becomes strong; under its influence he achieves things that would ordinarily be beyond his power; he leaves off his symptoms and seems apparently to have recovered – merely for the sake of the analyst. The analyst may shamefacedly admit to himself that he set out on a difficult undertaking without any suspicion of the extraordinary powers that would be at his command. (Freud, 1938: 125–6)

'Transference' is a fiction, invented and maintained by the therapist to protect himself from the consequences of his own behavior [...] Dependency is a built-in feature for the (client) at the beginning, and the treatment itself often promotes further dependency. The patient (or client) is typically anxious, distressed, in need of help, often lonely. The therapist, presumably, is not. Instead, he holds a professional role (especially if a physician) that ranks at or near the top in sociological surveys of romantic attractiveness to women seeking husbands (ahead of astronauts and other celebrities). The situation is set for intimacy, privacy, trust, frequent contact, revelation of precious secrets. Second, it is also the case that there is an ongoing search, on the part of most adolescents and adults, for sexual companionship. It requires only the opportunity for intimacy. One does not need to look into therapy for arcane and mysterious sources of erotic feelings. They are commonplace, everywhere, carried about from place to place. Psychotherapy will encounter sexual attraction as surely as it encounters nature. The simple combination of urge and situation is a formula for instant, if casual, romantic fantasy [...] Third, there is a supremely important special factor in a behavior to which all therapists subscribe and try to produce. It is *understanding*. Freud bluntly put it, (of transference) 'it is a kind of falling in love'. Let me put this bluntly too: *understanding is a form of love-making*. It may not be so intended, but that is one of its effects. [...] In this same context, *misunderstanding is a form of hate-making*. It works equally well since being misunderstood in a generally understanding relation is a shock, betrayal, frustration. (Shlien, 1984: 170–1)

Learning task

Read through these two passages, and decide which of these statements best reflects your own understanding and experience. Do you find some validity on both positions? If so, how would you seek to integrate or reconcile these different points of view? What are the implications, in terms of how a counsellor might work with a client, of the 'transference' and 'counter-theory' perspectives?

Putting theory to use: thinking about cases

Introduction

This section of the Workbook includes some brief case scenarios, describing clients who may make use of counselling services. With each of the cases, you may find it useful first of all to respond on the basis of your own intuitive or personal reactions and thoughts. Try to imagine that you are the counsellor to each of these clients, and do your best to enter in to the imaginary situation that is depicted.

Research into the sources of counsellors' emotional responses to clients is discussed on pages 96–7 of *An Introduction to Counselling*.

After you have written down your own personal response to the case, then you may find it helpful to look at it from the vantage point of theoretical perspectives that interest you: psychodynamic, cognitive-behavioural, person-centred, feminist, systemic, narrative, and so on. It may be useful to refer to the lists of key terms and concepts at the end of each of the relevant chapters in *An Introduction to Counselling*. For example, the key concepts list for psychodynamic counselling (pages 120–1) indicates the main ideas that a psychodynamic counsellor would employ when working with a clients: attachment, defence mechanisms, transference and counter-transference, stages of development. The other theory chapters (for example, person-centred, cognitive-behavioural) also include similar lists of key concepts.

Once you have worked through how you might make sense of the case from alternative theoretical standpoints, you are ready to consider a number of questions that are highly relevant to the task of developing your own personal approach as a counsellor:

(?) Which of the alternative analyses of the case seemed *most* helpful? Why?

(?) Which of the alternative analyses of the case seemed *least* helpful? Why?

(?) Which theoretical model, or combination of models, seemed to fit most closely with your own personal reading of the case?

(?) What do your answers to these questions say about you, and what you stand for as a counsellor?

It is possible to expand your awareness of both theoretical and practice issues by working on these case studies on your own. However, it can also be illuminating to discuss the cases in the context of a peer group of counsellors. It is probable that, in a group, you may find that your awareness of the issues presented by each of the case study clients may be significantly expanded, as different members of the group introduce their own perceptions, sensitivity and experience. This kind of group discussion can give a sense of what can happen in good supervision. What you may also find, however, is that you become more aware of the reality that each practitioner seems to make use of a somewhat limited palette of assumptions and emotions when responding to clients.

Student counselling: the case of Ms B

Ms B is 24 years old, single, and a university student in the final year of a social science degree. Throughout the course she has felt frustrated at the grades she has received, which have averaged around 50–55 per cent. Now, having returned in October, she finds herself worrying about her grades so much that she goes to the student counselling service. At the first meeting, the counsellor asks her to talk about what the problem is, and about the important things in her life that she feels might be associated with it.

The main points which emerge are:

–   She just feels herself to be a 'complete failure';

–   She was the oldest of four children and always felt under pressure to do well at school;

–   She was close to her grandmother, who died when she was 16;

–   She did not feel that she got enough support or encouragement from her parents, particularly when she did her university entrance exams;

–   The thought of going home to live with her parents after the degree is 'scary';

–   She failed to get good grades in her university entrance exams and worked in a shop for a year before doing an 'Access to University' course at a community college;

–   She is lonely, with no friends or boyfriend and finds it difficult to talk to her flatmates;

–   She has no idea what she is going to do after graduating. When asked what her ideal job would be, she pauses for several seconds and then answers that she would like to be a trainee manager with a large supermarket chain, but that she has no hope of getting a good enough degree for that, and 'anyway they only take really confident types';

–   She sees herself as overweight and eats too much chocolate;

–   She avoids writing essays and spends a lot of time reading novels rather than doing academic work;

–   She gets very anxious when she starts work on an essay, which makes it difficult to concentrate;

–   She finds it difficult to ask tutors what is wrong with her essays;

–   She only speaks in seminars when explicitly asked a question;

–   She is critical of some tutors for being unfair in their marking and not making sure that books are in the library;

–   When asked what her aim is for counselling, and what she would like to change, she first says that she's not sure, then after a few moments adds: 'I guess the biggest thing is being afraid of other people ... I just feel as if everyone is going to criticize me ... I can never relax with anyone';

–   The counsellor notices that Ms B seems distant and talks about herself in a detached manner;

–   Throughout the session, Ms B uses metaphors and images associated with fighting, such as 'It was a battle to get to University', and 'I retreat into my bed with a carton of ice cream';

– At the end of the session, the counsellor is aware of a strong feeling of sadness, and of wondering whether Ms B would come back for another session. The counsellor wondered whether he/she had somehow not been good enough for Ms B, and may have let her down in some way.

Consider the following questions:

(?) What are the main issues that Ms B is bringing to counselling?

(?) How would you describe the way that Ms B relates to the world? What kind of a world does she inhabit?

(?) Why now? What is the possible significance of choosing to visit the counselling service at this time?

(?) If you were her counsellor, what else would you be interested in knowing about Ms B, in future sessions?

(?) How would you work with Ms B? What would you be trying to do?

(?) How many sessions do you think Ms B would need? On what basis do you make this estimate?

A client's opening statement

What a person says first, at the beginning of their initial counselling session, can often encapsulate they key issues for which he or she is seeking help. It is important as a counsellor to be able to 'tune in' to a client from their first words.

The following statement was made by a young black man at the start of his first counselling session:

I was sitting in the room and waiting beforehand and I was thinking about why I was about seven or eight years old and I remember reading a book I believe I can't recall the name of this book by Jung, I think it was and I recall when I was reading that that at that time I used to go down the basement of my home and turn off all the lights and in a way that was kind of closing the outside world and concentrating on what I wanted to do and what I wanted to be. And at seven years-old I was I was into that and today I am in the same position really, you know, trying to find out what I want to do, what I want to be and I've learned a lot of things. I've learned a lot of things since I found out that I had leukemia which is about a year ago this June and I learned an awful lot of things … I think that I've listened for so long to other people about who I was and I remember in second grade I was a potential credit to my race that was one of the … I would always wonder why I couldn't be a credit to somebody else's race also but I think I really conditioned to be something, to be some kind of a symbol or whatever and not really being a person you know. I kind of missed out on my childhood to an extent you know I don't really regret it, I don't think I regret it anyway but I've really been through a lot of changes and I think that now after finding out I had the leukemia and after dealing with the leukemia in the way I did it's just really incredible, you see it was last June when I found out and I proceeded to get everything in order because I was told that I had less than a year to live and that was a trip and that was a trip and … and on one hand you know I accepted the death, you know at my young age I think I have lived long and a great deal, but that was the start of some things that, err, that really has had an affect on me today like I am much happier than I have ever been today, I am much happier, but there's some, there's a lot of hurt too … there's an awful lot of hurt and I think I am just beginning to realize that. Because, you know, in being a credit to your race in being an outstanding student, an outstanding scholar, an outstanding football player whatever leaves you little room to to be….

Consider the following questions:

 What feelings, emotions and images does this opening statement trigger in you?

 What is your sense of the key themes and issues in what this person is presenting?

 What would you say to this person at this point?

Further reading

This statement is taken from a case of Carl Rogers, filmed in 1977, and widely available on video. As with many of Rogers's recorded cases, the process of his work with this client has been subjected to careful analysis. A book containing a series of responses to this case, from a range of different writers, is available:

Moodley, R., Lago, C. and Talahite, C. (2004) *Carl Rogers Counsels a Black Client: Race and Culture in Person-centred Counselling*. Ross-on-Wye: PCCS Books.

Other cases involving Rogers are examined in:

Farber, B.A., Brink, D.C. and Raskin, P.M. (eds) (1996) *The Psychotherapy of Carl Rogers: Cases and Commentary*. New York: Guilford Press.

The case of Glenys – first session

You are working as a counsellor in a GP practice. One of the GPs refers Glenys to you. She has been making appointments to see the GP every week for more than two years, complaining of pains in her gut, and breathing difficulties. Glenys has been sent for extensive tests and specialist consultations, but no physical causes for her symptoms have been identified. The GP suggested that it might be helpful for Glenys to see the practice counsellor. The practice offers clients six sessions of counselling, with extension to 12 sessions with the permission of the GP. It has taken several weeks to find an appointment time that is suitable for Glenys. During this period she has continued to visit the GP.

Glenys is 45 years of age. She is married, with two children. Before her marriage, she worked as a care assistant in a home for the elderly. She took some time off when the children were small, and then returned to work. After gaining some qualifications, she now has a demanding job as the manager of a residential unit for people with learning difficulties.

At the first counselling session, Glenys walks into the room slowly, and doubles over, as if appearing to be in some pain. She is slightly built, and neatly dressed. She immediately engages in conversation, and starts to tell you about the various medical tests she has undergone and complementary therapies that she has tried out. She comes over as a very positive person, who is determined to get to the bottom of these health problems. It is difficult for you to get a word in edgeways. She talks quickly.

When asked about the situations that seem to bring about her symptoms, Glenys replies that both the pain and breathing difficulties are around most of the time, except when she goes to Spain on holiday. When asked about the worst recent episodes, she describes a couple of occasions at work, when she has had to deal with difficult staff meetings.

You invite Glenys to talk about the relationship with her husband and children. She describes these as wonderful: 'they are such a help to me'. She describes in some detail the accomplishments of her children and the qualities of her husband: 'he is a rock'. She uses very few feeling words.

Towards the end of the first session, you talk to Glenys about what counselling will involve. She vehemently denies that she is mentally ill, or that there is any psychological side to her difficulties. You explain that many people find it stressful to live with pain and other symptoms, and that counselling may help her with this. She replies that 'I will try anything that might help'.

Your impression of Glenys in this first meeting is of someone who is presenting a 'nice' face to the world, but who is concealing sides of herself that are perhaps not so 'nice'. You have a slight feeling of irritation, which you wonder might be the result of being forced to be a passive audience to Glenys's high speed monologues. You also have a sense of needing to handle her carefully.

Consider the following questions:

 What theoretical approaches might help you to make sense of the information you have about this client?

The following section describes the further progress of this case. It is recommended to respond to the questions in this section before reading about what happened next.

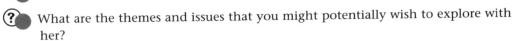 What approach might you take with Glenys?

What are the themes and issues that you might potentially wish to explore with her?

What might be the challenges involved in developing a relationship with this woman?

Are there any counselling methods or techniques that might be particularly relevant or effective?

The case of Glenys – later sessions

In the second and third sessions Glenys has talked at length about the situations in which her pain and breathing difficulties occur. Your impression is that she has thought deeply about the question you asked in the first session, and is perhaps trying to please you, or conform to your expectations, by working hard on this task.

At the start of the fourth session she excitedly tells you that, during the previous week, she had experienced a moment of 'really bad' breathing difficulties. She describes a staff meeting at work, where all the care staff and domestics were together to hear about some new arrangements about overtime payments and holidays. Some of them had become very angry, and directed their anger at her, even though her boss, the divisional manager, had also been present:

At one point I had to sit down, because I thought that I was going to have a heart attack. I was breathing very quickly, like it was out of control. My arms were sort of numb and tingly at the same time. I thought I was going to choke or faint. Everyone was very good. They told me I had been under a lot of stress, and brought me some water, and then the meeting went ahead. But I felt extremely shaky all day.

After saying this, Glenys quickly moves on to give her account of other situations during the week that had been associated with symptoms.

You feel convinced that the episode at the staff meeting was a panic attack.

Task for reflection

How might you work with these further developments on Glenys's life? What could you do to explore the meaning and experience of the panic attack for Glenys? Would you want to offer information or strategies that would help her to cope with such situations in future?

Session 7

Glenys was very pleased with the work you did together over the panic attacks: 'it has made a huge difference'. She fed this information back to the GP, who was very happy to agree to a further six sessions.

At the beginning of session 7, Glenys seems very agitated, and almost tearful. She begins to describe an occasion the previous day when she and her husband disagreed over how to respond to a demand from one of their children:

It was like a knife in my gut. Very painful, I had to take three of my pills. He just wasn't listening to me. He seemed too sure of what was right, and wouldn't allow me to get a word in at all. I felt like my tummy was really bloated and almost exploding. It was sort of the same as the pain that is usually there, but much more intense, and focused on one place. Later on I developed a headache and had to go to bed. I tried some yoga exercises, but it didn't do much good.

Your immediate sense is that Glenys has told you something that is very important, for her and for your relationship. You feel closer to her. It is the first time that she has ever been even slightly critical of her husband.

Task for reflection

What could you do to explore the meaning and experience of this pain episode for Glenys?

Session 11

Glenys is very aware that the counselling sessions have come to an end. You have referred her to the local NHS psychotherapy service, and she is on their waiting list (average waiting time: 15 months).

Up until now Glenys has talked almost entirely about events that have taken place within the last year. Today, she comes in and tells you that she has visited her father's grave. She had not mentioned her father before:

I don't know why I did it. I was just driving past the cemetery and the idea came to me. It was only when I found the headstone that I realized that it was virtually the anniversary of his death. I was only 12 when he died [tears]. He had been in trouble with some financial business at his work, and died in a car crash. It must have been suicide, but no-one ever talked about it. It was good to stand there on the hillside and just remember a few things about what he was like. He was a great dad [more tears]. He used to take me to gymnastics, even to competitions in England. I was so much into sport, it was what I wanted to do with my life. He was always around. My life was never the same afterwards. My mother needed so much help.

Task for reflection:

How might you work with this story? How might you respond to what Glenys has said? *Finally*, look back at all of your responses to the Glenys case:

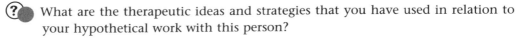 What are the therapeutic ideas and strategies that you have used in relation to your hypothetical work with this person?

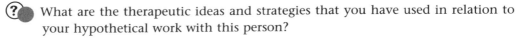 What does your sense of how you might work with this client say to you about your theoretical position as a counsellor?

'I hear these voices telling me what to do'

You are a counsellor working with a voluntary sector agency, which offers open-ended weekly counselling sessions to people with a wide variety of problems. There are no assessment screening or 'intake' interviews – the client phones up and makes an appointment, and the counsellor is the first person in the agency that they talk to.

Gary is in his mid-20s. He is neatly dressed, and seems rather nervous when he enters the counselling room. He walks to his chair slowly and deliberately, and does not engage in eye contact. When you ask him to say what has brought him to counselling, he replies: 'I hear these voices telling me what to do. It's getting so bad that my brother told me that I need to get some help'.

When invited to say more about what is happening in his life as a whole, it emerges that Gary lives at home with his parents. He mentions several times that he has a predictable routine, which he does not like to change. He has had a clerical job for many years, which involves minimal contact with the public. Recently, he has felt 'stressed out' by his father's illness (who been diagnosed with cancer). It seems as though the family dynamic has started to change – Gary has found himself being required to take a more active role in supporting his mother. He does not mention the 'voices' again, and you do not ask him about them. Gary has a 'needy' way of talking, and is highly sensitive, almost suspicious, about any suggestions or questions that you put to him.

Throughout the session, you have a sense of 'walking on eggshells', and being very careful to go at Gary's pace. At the end of the counselling session, you agree to see Gary again. You feel uncertain about how best to make sense of what happened in the session, and wondering about the significance of these 'voices'.

Learning tasks:

(?) What are the main themes or issues that this client is expressing?

(?) What therapeutic ideas and strategies might you find helpful in relation to your hypothetical work with Gary?

(?) How would you approach the issue of the 'voices'?

(?) How might you negotiate a therapeutic 'contract' with this client? What would you want to include in the contract?

(?) What does your sense of how you might work with this client say to you about your theoretical position as a counsellor?

Further reading

Romme, M. and Escher, S. (1993) *Making Sense of Voices*. London: Mind.

A case of work stress

You are working as a counsellor for an Employee Assistance Programme (EAP), which has a contract to provide brief (six session) counselling for staff of a major national financial services company.

Jeff (27) makes an appointment to see a counsellor. He tells you that he saw his GP earlier in the week about his depression. All the GP offered was pills, so Jeff decided to try the company EAP. He tells you that he has had a successful career as an IT analyst. He has a good salary and owns his own flat in town. He describes himself as 'devastated' because his partner of five years – Rita – has suddenly left him, to move in with another man.

In a flat tone, he responds to your question about how he feels:

I just keep thinking about it. I can't go to work at all. In fact I can't do anything but sit in the flat playing records and looking at photo albums. I don't want to speak to anyone. My parents, my brother, my best friend, have all been round to see me but I pretend I am not in. I feel hurt and betrayed and angry and depressed all at the same time. Some of the time I think that if I can't have her, then no-one should have her. I feel like ending it all. I feel so worthless and tired of this nightmare that I wish I could just go to sleep forever and forget about it all. It would be all over. I know that things weren't going too well between us. She kept telling me that I was locked up in my work and always seemed tired and irritable. But I had no idea that it could have been that bad. The company has been going through a merger, and it's like everyone has two jobs, at least, to do. It's not the sort of place that you want to be first out of the car park at 5.

Learning task

(?) How might you feel at this moment? How might you respond? What would you say?

(?) What themes and issues might you want to explore further?

(?) How might you structure the remaining 30 minutes of the session?

(?) Which theoretical models or techniques might be helpful in your work with this client over the remaining 5 sessions?

Finally:

(?) What have you learned, in thinking about your response to this case, about yourself as a counsellor?

(?) What does your sense of how you might work with this client say to you about your theoretical approach?

Reflecting on practice: challenges to therapeutic relationship

Section 4

Introduction

The task of evolving a personal approach as a counsellor is not merely a matter of adopting a particular theoretical orientation, or assembling an integration of different theoretical ideas. For many counsellors, the process of discovering who they are as therapists only really hits them when they are faced with critical issues *in practice*. The aim of this section of the Workbook is to present a series of activities that evoke practical dilemmas that are associated with underlying questions such as 'what kind of a counsellor do I want to be?' and 'what is the personal style, or way of being with others, that suits me best?'

You may find that some of the scenarios and dilemmas described in these activities are already familiar to you, from your work as a counsellor. In these cases, your response to the learning task may help you to reflect more fully on your response to that situation, or to begin to consider what your *preferred* response might be. Other scenarios and activities may be introducing situations that you may never have encountered in your actual work with clients. In these cases, you may be able to use the learning task to imagine, or rehearse, the ways in which you might approach such a situation when it does cross your path.

The series of tasks in this section begin with a set of activities that invite you to articulate and reflect on the moral choices and principles that you draw upon in guiding your work, and your life as a whole. The reason for beginning with moral issues is that counselling is a highly morally sensitive endeavour. People who come to see a counsellor are often struggling to make choices in their life, to decide what is 'right' for them to do. The counsellor is inevitably drawn close to the person's life, in a way that makes it possible for him or her to hurt or exploit, as well as to help, the person. If a counsellor does not have confidence in the moral stance which he or she is taking in relation to the counselling relationship, it is likely that he or she may be paralyzed, unable to continue to be open to the client's process. It is therefore important, as a counsellor, to be aware of one's own values and moral landscape. For most people, this is a difficult thing to do; we live in a culture in which there are many competing moral stances.

The moral basis of counselling is discussed on pages 382–4 of *An Introduction to Counselling*.

Other activities in this section reflect the huge diversity of counselling methods that are currently in use. Becoming more aware of where you stand in relation to these methods is a good way to explore your identity as a counsellor. Inevitably, all counsellors find themselves drawn towards certain techniques, client groups and modes of delivery, while avoiding others. Some of the learning tasks invite you to look beyond your fascination or disinterest and to consider what having these views *means* to you, in terms of who you are – or wish to be – as a counsellor.

Exploring moral values

What are the moral values that are most important for you? Your practice as a counsellor is inevitably embedded in your sense of what it means to be a 'good' human being. The issues and choices that some clients make will undoubtedly challenge that sense of what is 'good' or 'right'. A personal approach to counselling is, therefore, informed by an appreciation of your own moral positions, as well as a capacity to respect the moral positions taken by others.

The three exercises described here are designed to enable you to begin to explore your personal moral values.

Instructions

Sources of moral influence in your life. Take a piece of paper and draw a 'timeline', from your birth to present. Along this line, indicate the 'moral communities' that you have belonged to, at various stages in your life. A moral community could be an organized religion, such as the Roman Catholic Church or the communist party, or it could be a less formal network, such as 'the rugby club', 'my friends' or 'the feminism seminar group'. A moral community is any grouping that sets standards for its members about 'correct' beliefs and the 'right' way to do things. For each of the moral communities, add a label listing the core moral rules or values for which it stood. You may find that at particular points in your life you may have been a member of more than one community. Once you have completed the timeline, reflect on what you have learned, in relation to the consistent moral themes in your life, and the areas of moral tension or uncertainty.

Moral proverbs and sayings. A good way to begin to map out your personal moral beliefs is to think about the moral proverbs and sayings to which you make reference in everyday life. It is also of interest to identify, if you can, the person whom you heard saying these things to you in the first instance. For example, you may have heard your grandmother saying 'who does he think he is?', or 'men are only interested in one thing'. What do statements like these tell you about your moral values and beliefs?

Your vision of the good life. What would your ideal world be like? What would 'utopia' be for you? Take a few minutes to write about the characteristics of the good life, from your own individual perspective.

Once you have completed these three exercises, bring together what you have learned about your moral values by drawing a list of the values or 'virtues' that are of central importance in your life.

Further reading

Compare your list of values with the discussion on pages 386–7 in *An Introduction to Counselling*, specifically the *theistic-humanistic* distinction, and the list of 'counsellor virtues' on page 395.

To place your reflections in a broader context, you might wish to read Tjeltveit, A. (1998) *Ethics and Values in Psychotherapy*. London: Routledge.

The implications of your moral values for your approach as a counsellor

The moral values and virtues that you espouse may help to shape the approach you take as a counsellor, in a variety of ways. For each of the dimensions of practice listed here, write some notes on the possible implications that might arise from your moral position. For example, if aesthetic/artistic values are highly significant for you, then this may imply developing a theoretical approach that makes space for creativity, working in a setting that allows art therapy methods to be employed and so on. If socialist and egalitarian values are significant, there may be quite different implications in terms of theoretical choice and work setting. You may find that your individuality as a counsellor arises from the ways that you have found in order to balance or reconcile different values in your own practice.

Theoretical orientation. Different theoretical orientations tend to emphasize different values, such as rationality, individual autonomy, spirituality, and so on. For you, what are the links between your values and moral position, and the theories of counselling that have meaning for you? It may be that certain theories allow you a vehicle fully to expressing your values fully. Alternatively, there may be areas of tension: a theoretical model may make a lot of sense to you in most respects, but there can nevertheless be specific ways in which it is hard to align it with some of your moral beliefs.

Way of working as a counsellor. There are many practical issues in counselling that reflect value choices. Some of these issues include: setting a limit to the number of sessions that a client can receive, charging fees, seeing a client individually or in a family context. Where do you stand on these matters?

Client groups. Are there client groups that you are drawn towards, that you get great satisfaction from? Are there groups of clients who are difficult for you to accept, or whose values are hard for you to appreciate and understand?

Practice setting. In what ways do your values influence the types of counselling settings within which you choose to work? For example, do you practice on a volunteer, unpaid basis, or in a paid job, or both? In what ways might the values of your colleagues matter to you? The values of organizational contexts may differ too – for example, some counselling agencies are grounded in religious commitment, while others embrace rational, 'evidence-based' practice. How much do these factors matter to you?

Once you have reflected on these practice domains, and written some notes in response to the questions outlined earlier, spend some time looking at the totality of your response: what have you learned about your own values, and about the relationships between these values and your counselling practice?

> The idea that different theories of counselling reflect alternative 'images of the person' is discussed on pages 36–7 and 52–3 of *An Introduction to Counselling*. Modes of delivery in counselling are discussed in Chapter 17. The issue of fee-paying is explored on pages 316–8.

What is your personal philosophy?

Arthur Combs was an American psychologist who worked with Carl Rogers in the 1950s. His research looked mainly at one of the fundamental notions of early client-centred therapy – that effective counselling was essentially a matter of possessing an appropriate attitude or philosophy of life, and conveying this to clients. For Combs (1986), the key elements of the counsellor's attitude were:

Beliefs about significant data. Good helpers are people-oriented. They seem to attend to internal personal meanings rather than external behavioural data and tune in to how things seem from the point of view of those with whom they work.

Beliefs about people. Effective helpers seem to hold more positive beliefs about the people they work with than do less effective helpers. They see them as trustworthy, able, dependable and worthy. They display co-operative rather than adversarial relationship attitudes: helper and client are on the same side of the fence. They perceive others as having the capacity to deal with their problems, and have faith that they can find adequate solutions, as opposed to doubting the capacity of people to handle themselves and their lives. Others are essentially dependable rather than undependable. They have confidence in the stability and reliability of others and no need to be suspicious of them.

Beliefs about self. The counsellor has a positive view of self, confidence in one's abilities, and a feeling of oneness with others, identifies with people, rather than sets self apart from them and tends to see self as a part of all mankind. Enough rather than wanting – self as having what is needed to deal with problems, rather than as lacking or unable to cope with problems. He/she has a willingness to disclose or share things about self – feelings and shortcomings are important and significant rather than needing to be hidden or covered up.

Beliefs about purposes or priorities. Good helpers tend to see events in terms of wider meanings and perspectives, from a broad rather than narrow perspective. They are concerned with the implications of events, rather than merely with the immediate and specific. They are not exclusively concerned with details but can perceive beyond the immediate to future and larger horizons.

Learning task

Reflect on the following questions:

 To what extent do your basic beliefs or personal philosophy correspond with the pattern that Combs views as associated with effective counselling?

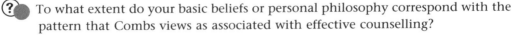 Do you believe that Combs's model is necessarily correct? Some would argue that he takes an over-optimistic and romantic view of the world, and that there are other 'world-views' that can also be found in successful counsellors.

Further reading

Combs, A. (1990) *A Theory of Therapy*. London: Sage.

Fear, R. and Woolfe, R. (1996) Searching for integration in counselling practice, *British Journal of Guidance and Counselling*, 24:399–412.

Moral dilemmas presented by clients

To a large extent, developing a personal approach to counselling is a matter of learning from experience. Things happen in counselling, clients turn up, that challenge your beliefs and assumptions, and force you, as a counsellor, to acknowledge what it is you stand for.

The brief client vignettes on this page include situations that are not straightforward for *any* counsellor. How would *you* respond to these clients? For each vignette, make some notes around the key practical and moral issues, as you perceive them, and around the possible courses of action that you might pursue in each case. What would you do?

Sam is a client referred by one of the GPs in the primary health clinic in which you are employed as a counsellor as a member of the primary care mental health team. The brief referral note that you have received states that Sam is undergoing a lot of stress and needs help to deal with his anxiety. Sam comes in to your office and begins by saying:

I need to get this off my chest. It's no good even starting to talk about anything until I have made this clear. I need help because I am in court in six weeks because I had sex with my partner's eight-year old daughter. She threw me out of the house and called the police. I just feel awful. I can't function at work at all. Everyone thinks I am just a piece of dirt. I keep thinking about it all the time.

Eva and Dave are clients in a marriage/couple counselling agency in which you work as a volunteer counsellor. They have already attended for three sessions, and have talked mainly about the arguments they have been having around whether they should stay together. Both of them feel, for different reasons, that the 'spark' has gone out of their relationship. At the start of the fourth session, Eva begins to talk about the way that Dave controls money. He sees himself as the breadwinner, and only gives Eva a fixed amount of money each week to run the household. Eva does not have a bank account in her own name, or any access to money without asking Dave. She turns to you and asks: 'this isn't right, is it?'. How do you reply to Eva?

Gina is a university student, who has been using the counselling service off and on throughout her course. She is in the second year of a degree. She has talked a lot about how her parents have always been emotionally distant, and divorced when she was 12, each of them starting new lives with different partners and starting new families. She believes that other people do not like her, and complains that she has no 'real friends'. Now she seems to have reached an impasse regarding her university work. Things have not been going well and she has fallen behind. She seems very depressed. In your most recent session, she talked a bit about how she sometimes cuts herself. On the evening following that session, she sends you an email in which she writes that she is feeling worse than ever.

What are the moral values that are evoked for you by each of these cases? What are the moral principles that you might refer to when arriving at a solution or strategy in response to the needs of these clients? Which of these cases would be *most* and *least* difficult for you? Why?

Ethical decision-making

Chapter 15 of *An Introduction to Counselling* provides an outline of the ethical principles that can be used as a guide for the practice of counselling. The websites of counselling organizations such as the British Association for Counselling and Psychotherapy (BACP) also carry detailed codes of ethical practice.

Use this material, and any other sources available to you, to formulate your decisions in relation to the following ethical dilemmas:

1. A client has been in counselling for a year, and has made great progress. She brings in an expensive gift for you. She knows that this is something that you would like, and she knows that you know that she would know this.

2. You have been counselling someone for six months who has a serious medical condition. You have a similar medical problem yourself. At the start of counselling you decided not to mention your similar health problem to the client. However, now you are finding it extremely difficult to carry on with the counselling, because what the client is talking about reminds you of your own pain, and you keep wanting to cry during sessions.

3. You are a counsellor in a school. The rule is that any children under 16 need to have parental permission to see you. You have just finished a group workshop for a class of 15-year-old children, on relationship skills. At the end one of them comes up to you and launches into the story of her problems. When asked, she says that her parents would never give her permission to see you officially.

4. You work in a counselling agency where you have a first assessment session with a client and then decide whether to offer them counselling or refer elsewhere. During the first assessment meeting with this client, you realize that: (a) his problem is within the remit of the service, (b) he is motivated to use counselling, and (c) you find him physically threatening and intimidating.

5. You have been counselling a couple for some time. You all decide that it would be useful to have a couple of individual sessions, where you see the husband and wife separately. In the first individual session with the wife she tells you that she has been having an affair but that she does not want you to tell her husband.

6. You have been counselling a couple for some time, and it is clear that they have serious relationship difficulties. At the time of the appointment only the wife turns up. The phone rings. It is the husband. He tells you that he has moved his belongings out of the house, and the marriage is over. He asks you to convey this information to his wife.

7. For some time you have been struggling to find a publisher for a book you want to write. It emerges that a client is a senior executive in a major publishing house. Her professional advice would be invaluable to you. In passing, at the end of a session she mentions, 'if you ever need any help getting a book published...'.

8. After a long day seeing several clients, you use your partner as a 'sounding board' to talk through aspects of the work, but without disclosing details of the identity of any of your clients.

9. With a client, you consistently feel a pull of sexual attraction.

10 At the end of a session, a client asks you for a hug.

11 At the end of a session, a client asks you to kiss him/her on the lips.

12 It is a late evening session, which has been a difficult and harrowing for the client. She has no car, and has to walk through deserted inner-city streets.

13 A client you have worked with for a long time, in private practice, is terminally ill. He asks if you would continue to see him in the hospice.

14 You are a counsellor in a rural area where everyone knows everyone else. How do you deal with confidentiality?

15 You are a student counsellor in a university. The counselling service is grossly under-resourced, but you try to do the best you can. You feel strongly that people in need should not be shunted on to a waiting list. You start to see clients during lunch breaks, and stay late in the evening. One week, you add up that you have seen 34 clients.

16 You work for a counselling agency that is highly sensitive to ethical issues. After several stormy staff meetings, it is decided that, to ensure informed consent, any people applying for counselling need to be informed, during their assessment interview, of all the alternative treatments that might exist for their problem, including drug treatment, exercise regimes and meditation.

Questions for further reflection:

What have you learned about yourself, your values, and your approach to counselling, from this exercise?

What are the implications of these dilemmas, in terms of the supervision, support and consultation that you require in order to work effectively as a counsellor?

Deconstructing the meaning of confidentiality

The principle of confidentiality represents an essential aspect of counselling. It is clear that counselling is a conversation or meeting that takes place *for* the person who is the client, rather than to compile any kind of report that might be handed on to a third party. However, much of the time the significance of confidentiality is largely taken for granted. Confidentiality is interpreted as being about making sure that client records are kept safe, the fact that the client is attending a therapy clinic is not made known to others, and so on. This activity invites you to develop a fuller appreciation of the idea of confidentiality.

Instructions

Over the space of a few days, carry out a personal inquiry into the meaning of confidentiality. Some of the inquiry tasks that you might attempt are:

1. Look up the meanings of confidentiality contained in the Oxford English Dictionary. Pay attention to the origins of this term. What does the etymology of the word tell you about some of the hidden, or implicit, meanings associated with the ways in which the word 'confidential' is used in both everyday and professional conversations.

2. Imagine that you are going to see a counsellor for the first time. What are your expectations or needs around confidentiality? What are your fears? Are there any questions that you want to ask your counsellor concerning confidentiality? Do you expect him or her to bring up the issue? What do you expect them to say? What would happen if you came away from that first meeting with doubts about the capacity of the counsellor to respect the confidentiality of information about you?

3. What kind and level of confidentiality might you expect from other people with whom you might talk about your personal problems, for example your best friend, a close family member, your priest or minister, your doctor? In what ways is counselling confidentiality different from 'confiding' in these other people? If counselling confidentiality is different from these other sorts of confidentiality, then why does it need to be so?

4. A person who has been sexually abused may, at some point, spend three therapy hours telling their counsellor the detailed story of what happened to them. The same person may spend three hours with a police officer relating the same story, for legal purposes. The psychological and emotional significance of these two 'tellings' is almost certainly very different. What part does confidentiality play in this difference?

5. Interview colleagues about their experience of confidentiality breaches. Have they ever, when in the role of client or service user, known or suspected that their confidentiality had been breached? How did they feel and what did they do? Have they ever, in the role of practitioner, intentionally or unwittingly breached the confidentiality of a client?

6. Consider the confidentiality guidelines from three professional codes of ethics, reproduced on pages 389–90 of *An Introduction to Counselling*. In the light of what you have found in your inquiry, how adequate are these statements?

There may be many other inquiry strategies that you might pursue – the ones listed here are merely suggestions. Once you have reached a sense of closure in relation to your inquiry, write a summary statement of your understanding of the meaning and significance of confidentiality in counselling.

Touching and being touched

The question of whether it is valuable, or acceptable, to touch clients (or be touched by them) has been widely debated within the counselling and psychotherapy profession. The position that a practitioner takes in relation to touch can be highly significant in defining his or her personal approach. On the one hand, some therapists within the humanistic tradition would argue that touch is a basic and fundamental form of human contact and communication, and if clients are to 'come to their senses', touch will need to be involved at some point. On the other hand, some psychoanalytic and psychodynamic therapists would regard touching as deeply mistaken, reflecting a violation of the boundary between client and therapist. Some classical analysts, sitting at the head of a couch, situate themselves so that the patient cannot see them, never mind touch them.

The following questions are designed to allow you to begin to map out your position in relation to touch:

1 What are your own 'personal rules' about touching and being touched? Under what circumstances do you appreciate being physically 'in touch' with another person? What feelings do you associate with touch? What are the different meanings associated with touch around different parts of your body, or the other person's body?

2 It is possible to analyse counsellor-client touching into different categories (Tune, 2001). Touch can be initiated either by the client or by the counsellor. Touch can take place at three times:

➡ Before the sessions (for instance, on the way to the counselling room – shaking hands on arrival);

➡ During the session (for example, putting an arm round a client who is in distress);

➡ After the session (touching the client's shoulder on the way out of the room).

Which of these categories of touch do you engage in, or could imagine yourself engaging in? To what extent does this depend on the client? Are there categories of client who are, for you, 'touchable' or 'out of touch'?

3 What are the dilemmas that you have come across, or can imagine coming across, in respect of client-counsellor touch within your own practice?

> Issues around the use of touch in counselling are explored on pages 406–10 of *An Introduction to Counselling*. A discussion of the wider theme of embodiment can be found on pages 52–3.

Make some notes to record your reflections in response to these questions. Try to sum up your conclusions, in terms of your personal approach to touching in counselling. To what extent, and in what ways, might your personal position be in accordance with, or in conflict with, the 'rules for touching' implicitly or explicitly adopted by the theoretical model, workplace or training course within which you operate?

Further reading

Hunter, M. and Struve, J. (1998) *The Ethical Use of Touch in Psychotherapy*. Thousand Oaks, CA: Sage.

Making sense of stories

Sensitivity and awareness in relation to stories is a key skill in any kind of counselling practice. There are two kinds of story that clients tell, or refer to, in counselling sessions:

➡ Stories about actual events or incidents that happened in the person's life. These are concrete, specific accounts of what took place, who was involved, and what the person felt. Typically, clients tell five or six such stories during the course of a therapy session;

➡ Stories about other people, that have meaning for the client. These may often be fictional stories, such as fairytales, novels or films, or religious stories. This kind of story is mentioned less often in therapy sessions, but can often be highly significant.

In recent years, a substantial amount of research has been carried out into the significance of the stories that clients tell in therapy. Some key principles have emerged from these studies:

1 *The story reflects the typical pattern of relationships in the person's life.* The interplay of relationships within the stories that a person tells, or in which the person is interested, can often reflect the pattern of relationships in that person's life as a whole. For instance – does the person tell stories of being alone, being in two-person relationships, being in three-person relationships and so on? Lester Luborsky (Luborsky and Crits-Christoph, 1990) has suggested that stories have an underlying structure in terms of how the person expresses his or her needs in relation to others. He argues that any story can be analysed in terms of the *wish* of the person, the *response of the other*, and the *response of self*. The types of wishes, responses of other, and responses of self that a person expresses appear to be fairly consistent across all, or most, of the stories that he or she tells.

> The work of Lester Luborsky is discussed on pages 227–30 and 465–6 of *An Introduction to Counselling.*

2 *The story conveys the person's image of the world that he or she lives in.* What kind of environment is described? Is the world that is evoked by the story a place that is safe, where people's needs are met, or is it a hostile and dangerous world?

3 *The story expresses, or triggers in the listener, the emotions that are significant for the teller.* What are the feelings that are associated with different characters in the story? How do you feel, as a listener, when hearing or reading the story?

In the *Your favourite story* exercise, in Section 1 of the Workbook, you were invited to identify and summarize a favourite story from your own life. Apply the three principles above to that story. In what ways does your favourite story encapsulate the key emotional and relationship themes in your life? What have you learned about yourself from reflecting on this story in these terms? In what ways might you envisage being able to use these ideas in order to listen more fully to the meanings embedded in the stories that your clients are telling you?

If you chose a fairy story as your favourite story, you may be interested in considering the special significance of this kind of narrative. The psychoanalyst Bruno Bettelheim (1976), and the founder of Transactional Analysis, Eric Berne (1975), along with many other therapists, have suggested that fairytales embody basic human life-scripts.

Moreover, because fairy stories are heard by a child early in life, they have the potential to act as a kind of 'template' for the development of personality throughout a child's later development.

Further reading

Information about different approaches to analysing clients' narratives can be found in:

Angus, L.E. and McLeod, J. (eds) (2004) *Handbook on Narrative and Psychotherapy: Practice, Theory and Research*. Thousand Oaks, CA: Sage.

Book, H. (2004) The CCRT approach in working with patient narratives in psychodynamic psychotherapy, in L. Angus and J. McLeod (eds) *Handbook of Narrative and Psychotherapy: Practice, Theory and Research*. Thousand Oaks, CA: Sage.

McLeod, J. (1997) *Narrative and Psychotherapy*. London: Sage.

The meaning of boundary

The idea that relationships between people can be understood in terms of *boundaries* has had wide application within the domain of counselling and psychotherapy. The notion of boundary implies that there is a limit beyond which a person should not go in their relationship with the other. Venturing beyond that limit is a 'violation' or 'transgression' that may express something about the motivation of the violator.

There is much debate between therapists concerning the implications of the use of the idea of *boundary* in counselling practice. It is important to keep in mind that 'boundary' is a metaphor, which – like any metaphor – highlights some aspects of a phenomenon while concealing others.

This learning activity invites you to examine the meaning of the term 'boundary' in your own life, through the following questions:

 What are the boundaries that you draw in your own everyday life? What are the qualities or characteristics of these boundaries? How would anyone know that a boundary existed for you? How would they know when they had transgressed that boundary?

 A 'boundary' can be defined as the edge of a territory or space – where that territory meets another territory. What other words or images do you use to refer to this kind of phenomenon (for example: wall, barrier, fence, interface, line and so on)?

 When you meet another person for the first time, what do you do to establish your mutual boundaries?

 With someone you have known for some time, how do boundaries become re-negotiated or re-defined?

 What kind of boundary do you seem to need, in different situations? (Boundaries can be strong or weak, flexible or rigid, permeable or impermeable.)

The debate over the concept of boundary is reviewed on pages 311–3 of *An Introduction to Counselling*.

Once you have explored your personal experience of boundaries in your everyday life, look at the implications of what you have learned for how you are (or how you would wish to be) as a counsellor.

What does 'counselling' mean to people in your community?

One of the fundamental ideas in *An Introduction to Counselling* is that, in modern society, counselling is characterized by diversity and multiple perspectives. Counselling is not a single, unitary activity – there are many different approaches and types of counselling. To understand what counselling is, it is therefore necessary to appreciate the contours and implications of this diversity. This activity provides an opportunity to begin to map out the various shades of meaning of the term 'counselling', both in the community or city in which you live, and in the wider culture of which that community is a part.

Tasks

➡ Where does 'counselling' (defined broadly, to include both formal and informal sources of 'therapy') take place in your community? Make a list of all the sources of 'counselling' that you can discover.

➡ What do the words 'counselling' and 'psychotherapy' mean to people? Ask four or five people you know for their definitions of these terms.

➡ What do words like counselling, counseling, psychotherapy and self-help produce from an Internet search?

➡ Over the course of a week, make a note of the use of counselling 'news' and 'therapy jargon' in the media (newspapers, magazines, films, television).

➡ Collect examples of jokes and cartoons about counselling and psychotherapy.

Once you have collected enough material on the social and cultural meanings of 'counselling' and 'psychotherapy' use it as a basis for reflecting on the following issues:

? What has your research taught you about the state of counselling today?

? What do people know about counselling? What are their fantasies?

? What are the key themes in people's views of counselling?

? How positive is the public perception of counselling? What are the areas of public misunderstanding of counselling and therapy that you have come across?

? What might be the possible sources of this confusion?

? To what extent do the findings of your research support (or contradict) the views and themes outlined in Chapters 1 and 2 of *An Introduction to Counselling*?

? What is your impression about what could be changed to make counselling more relevant or accessible to people?

? What do people want when they visit a counsellor?

Writing letters

A constant issue in counselling is the person's relationship with 'significant others' in his or her life. From a narrative perspective, people can often become 'stuck' in their lives by repeating the same 'old story' over and over again to other people close to them.

One useful way of helping people to review, and if necessary change, these stories is to invite them to write letter to this other person. Typically, these letters are never sent, or maybe the final one from a series of letters is sent, with the earlier letters (angry, confused, despairing) being retained in a diary or destroyed.

Clients may be invited to write a letter during a counselling session, but more usually write in their own time and bring the letter in the next time they see their therapist. Letter writing is often used by bereavement counsellors – for example writing to someone who has died.

The aim of this learning activity is to give you an opportunity to explore the experience of therapeutic letter-writing

Instructions

Think of someone in your life who is, or has been, important to you, but with whom there are currently some unresolved issues. This could be someone you have fallen out with, someone who has moved away to live in another place, or someone who has died.

Give yourself at least 45 minutes to write a letter to this person. Do not censor what you write – this letter will never be sent. Keep writing down *everything* that you might possibly wish to say to this person – positive as well as negative. Once you have finished writing the letter, put it in a safe place.

Some examples of the use of letter-writing in therapy can be found on pages 235–40 of *An Introduction to Counselling*.

One or two days after your letter-writing episode, take some time to consider the following questions:

(?) How did you feel when you were writing the letter? What was the experience like for you?

(?) Have your thoughts, feelings and attitude towards the letter-recipient changed? In what ways?

(?) Do you now wish to read the letter again? What do you want to do with it? Is there anyone you would like to ask to read the letter?

(?) Has the writing of this letter been helpful or beneficial for you, or unhelpful and destructive? Or both?

(?) What are the therapeutic processes that took place?

Finally:

(?) What have you learned about the relevance of therapeutic letter-writing for your own approach to counselling?

(?) What further training, research or supervision might you need in order to become competent in this way of working with clients?

The therapeutic use of reading

One of the techniques that has always been used by people to sort out their problems is to get insight and advice through reading. For example, in the latter half of the nineteenth century there was a huge market in 'self-improvement' books, particularly in the USA. Probably everyone has their favourite novel (or even children's story) that means a lot to them.

Although some counsellors and psychotherapists have always recommended books to their clients, it is only recently that this practice has received much attention in terms of theory and research. This learning activity invites you to think about the extent to which therapeutic reading (self-help books or 'bibliotherapy') might form part of your personal approach as a counsellor.

Learning task

Visit a public library and examine the section with self-help books. Most of these will be for medical conditions, but some will concentrate on psychological problems such as assertiveness, depression, and so on. Look through these books to get a sense of what they have to offer and then choose *one* book to read, preferably on a topic that has some personal meaning for you.

> The therapeutic use of reading is discussed on pages 443–59 An Introduction to Counselling.

When reading the self-help book, consider these questions:

 How helpful do you think this book would be? Would you recommend it to a client?

 Who would find it useful?

 What makes it helpful or unhelpful?

 What are the model or models of therapy that it is promoting? For example, is it essentially offering common-sense advice, psychodynamic insights, or some other approach?

 Are there any ways in which, in your opinion, the book might be dangerous or misleading?

 What are the advantages and disadvantages of using this book, when compared to face-to-face counselling?

You might also find it interesting to do an Internet search on 'self-help', or follow up the reviews and discussion of recently-published self-help books on the Amazon bookshop website (you can even send in your thoughts on the book you have read as a contribution to Amazon).

Final questions:

 What are the characteristics of good self-help books, in your view? Are stories of how others had overcome similar problems most helpful, or is it better to provide structured learning routines? How important is it for self-help materials to have a spiritual dimension?

(?) What are the practical implications of integrating the use of self-help reading materials into your counselling practice? For example: at what point do you recommend a book and how do you link the book into what happens in face-to-face sessions?

(?) How useful might movies be, as an alternative to self-help books? Which films could you imagine using? People typically become more emotionally involved in movies – is this helpful or not?

Further reading

Cohen, L. (1994) Phenomenology of theraputic reading, with implications for research and practice of bibliotherapy, *The Arts in Psychotherapy*, 21:37–44.

Fuhriman, A., Barlow, S. and Wanlass, J. (1989) Words, imagination, meaning: towards change, *Psychotherapy*, 26:149–60.

Counselling in the media

Magazine problem pages ('agony aunts') and TV shows such as Oprah Winfrey probably represent the most widely-used forms of 'counselling' in Western societies. However, are these outlets providing experiences that are genuinely therapeutic, or are they merely forms of entertainment?

Learning tasks

➡ Analyse what you find in the problem pages of at least two contrasting publications (e.g. one from a serious newspaper and one from a popular women's magazine). What kind of advice do they give? What types of problems are addressed? What are the therapeutic processes that could be taking place?

➡ Analyse, in a similar fashion, some television shows in which personal problems are explored.

Once you have collected some material on media counselling, consider the following questions:

? How helpful do you think these outlets might be for those who use them? Would you recommend them, or use them yourself?

? Who seems to make use of these forms of help? Are they the same people who make use of counselling?

? What are the helpful and unhelpful aspects of 'media therapy'?

? What are the model or models of therapy that are being promoting? For example, are they essentially offering behaviourist advice, or psychodynamic insights, or some other approach?

? What are the advantages and disadvantages when compared to face-to-face counselling?

? Are there any ways in which they might be dangerous or misleading?

? If asked, would you host a TV show of this kind, or edit a problem page? If not, why not?

? How should professional counselling associations respond to the growth of 'media therapy'?

On-line counselling

One of the basic assumptions or cherished 'truths' held by the vast majority of counsellors and psychotherapists is that the quality of the therapeutic relationship is crucial to success in therapy. But what happens when client and counsellor never meet each other?

Most therapists believe that counselling 'at a distance' (e.g. using telephone, letter or email) may be necessary in emergencies (e.g. crisis helplines such as the Samaritans) but can never achieve the depth and meaningfulness of conventional face-to-face therapy. However, in recent years email has increasingly been used as a medium for therapy.

Some of the issues raised by on-line counselling are discussed on pages 442–3 of *An Introduction to Counselling*.

Reflect on your own experience with email:

 Do you ever use it for 'therapeutic' purposes (e.g. with friends)? How effective is this for you? For you personally, what are the advantages and disadvantages of email when compared to talking to someone face-to-face?

Spend some time searching the Internet for on-line counselling services.

 How helpful and trustworthy do these services appear to you?

 How do you imagine you might feel, as a potential client, using such a service for the first time – what might be your hopes and fears?

 What are the challenges that you might imagine as an on-line counsellor? What new or different skills might you require?

Finally, in terms of the on-line counselling that you have examined, what do you believe could be the opportunities and also the limitations of email therapy?

Further reading

Goss, S. and Anthony, K. (eds) (2003) *Technology in Counselling and Psychotherapy: a Practitioner's Guide*. London: Palgrave Macmillan.

Lange, A., Schoutrop, M., Schrieken, B. and Ven, J-P. (2002) Interapy: a model for therapeutic writing through the internet, in S.J. Lepore and J.M. Smyth (eds) *The Writing Cure: How Expressive Writing Promotes Health and Emotional Well Being*. Washington: American Psychological Association.

Indoors or outdoors? Using nature in therapy

Traditionally, influenced by the example of the doctor-patient consultation, counselling and psychotherapy sessions have taken place in offices. The content of therapy sessions has generally focused on either interpersonal problems that have been troubling the client, or difficulties the person has been having in regulating their thoughts and feelings.

In recent years, some practitioners have started to challenge these assumptions, in arguing that the relationship of a person with *nature* represents a crucial dimension of well-being, and that finding ways of bringing nature into the therapeutic process can be highly beneficial.

Enviromentalism is briefly discussed on page 525 of *An Introduction to Counselling*, and the significance of physical place on page 251.

One approach to the use of nature is to hold therapy sessions out of doors, for example in a wilderness area. Another approach is to invite the client to consider their relationship with nature, and to examine the link between that relationship and the problems they are experiencing in their life. Burns (1998) has devised a simple technique for facilitating this process, which he has called the *Sensory Awareness Inventory*. The client is given a piece of paper divided into six labelled columns: sight, sound, smell, taste, touch and activity. They are then instructed: 'under each heading, please list 10–20 items or activities from which you get pleasure, enjoyment or comfort'. What the client has written can be used in therapy in different ways. The client can be asked simply to consider what he or she has learned about him/herself from completing the exercise. Typically, clients report that there are many sources of sensory pleasure, enjoyment and comfort that they have been neglecting in their life, and which would be valuable to restore or expand. Following further exploration, connections may often be made between personal problems and the absence of nature-based experience.

Activities

How relevant is working in, and with nature, for your practice, and your personal approach as a counsellor? What are the advantages and disadvantages that you imagine might be associated with seeing clients out of doors?

Try the *Sensory Awareness Inventory* for yourself. What did you discover about yourself? Could these discoveries be of potential value in your therapy?

If you find, arising from these reflections, that nature-influenced work is attractive and meaningful for you, then also consider: what are the theoretical implications of working in this way?

How to be really ineffective

Research studies into the outcomes of therapy have found that a substantial number of people with psychological problems get better without making use of professional help, and that there is a wide range of levels of effectiveness across therapists. Some counsellors and psychotherapists appear to get good results with almost every client they see, while other practitioners may only generate a good outcome with around 30 per cent of their clients.

These issues were recognized by the family therapist Jay Haley (1969):

What has been lacking in the field of therapy is a theory of failure. Many clinicians have assumed that any psychotherapist could fail if he wished. However, recent studies of the outcome of therapy indicate that spontaneous improvement of patients is far more extensive than was previously realized. There is a consistent finding that between fifty and seventy percent of patients on waiting list control groups not only do not wish treatment after the waiting list period but have really recovered from their emotional problems … Assuming that these findings hold up in further studies, a therapist who is incompetent and does no more than sit in silence and scratch himself will have at least a fifty percent success rate with his patients. How then can a therapist be a failure?

In an attempt to develop a comprehensive theory of therapeutic failure, Haley identified 12 key factors. There is not space to summarize all of the Haley model here. However, the first factor conveys the gist of his analysis:

The central pathway to failure is based upon a nucleus of ideas which, if used in combination, make success as a failure almost inevitable:

Step A: Insist that the problem which brings the patient into therapy is not important. Dismiss it as merely a 'symptom' and shift the conversation elsewhere…

Step B: Refuse to treat the presenting problem directly. Offer some rationale, such as the idea that symptoms have 'roots', to avoid treating the problem…

Step C: Insist that if a presenting problem is relieved, something worse will develop. This myth makes it proper not to know what to do about symptoms and will even encourage patients to cooperate by developing a fear of recovery.

How far do you agree with Haley's analysis of the process of therapeutic failure? Do you agree with him that an understanding of failure is an essential element of any approach to counselling? What is your own theory of failure, in terms of your own work as a counsellor? How do you explain failure?

This research is summarized on pages 456–60 and page 481 of *An Introduction to Counselling*.

Developing a professional identity: putting it all together

Introduction

The aim of this section of the Workbook is to provide some opportunities for reflecting on the questions and activities in earlier sections, and arriving at an overview of your identity as a counsellor. There are perhaps two main dimensions to this process: summing up and looking ahead.

The exercises in the Workbook have involved exploring many different aspects of what is involved in being a counsellor. Learning about counselling is an open-ended commitment: there is always more to be known, new edges of awareness, surprises.

> It is recommended that you leave the activities in this section to the end — they build on your responses to activities in earlier sections of the Workbook.

But it is also likely that you may have used the Workbook at a stage in your career where learning and development have been a primary focus, and are set to move into another stage in which application and practice are more central. It can be useful, at this point of transition, to take stock of what you have learned, in the sense of being clear about your achievements and resources. Moreover, by documenting these achievements and resources (for example by writing and keeping your reflections on the tasks in this section) you are creating a statement about 'where you are now' to which you may wish to return at some point in the future. Summing up and taking stock can also contribute to a sense of closure at the end of training. Many training programmes and courses require students to assemble a self-evaluation statement at the end of the course, which is then reviewed by tutors and fellow course members. The exercises in this section of the Workbook are no substitute for such an assignment, but may still be useful in stimulating self-reflection around relevant themes.

This final section also looks ahead, at the future possibilities and next steps in your journey as a counsellor, in relation to the type of work you might do, and the further training and personal development that might be helpful. Becoming a counsellor is about more than learning theory and skills and acquiring practical experience. It is about evolving a professional identity, a sense of who you are in your work. Hopefully, by the time you have completed this Workbook, the outline of that professional identity, and its basis in who you are as a person, should be at least beginning to be more consistently visible.

Reviewing your skills and qualities as a counsellor

The aim of this exercise is to give you an opportunity to draw some conclusions from the exercises you have completed in the Workbook. Reflect on the various learning tasks with which you have engaged in the Workbook, and also on other sources of learning concerning yourself as a counsellor (for instance, courses you have attended, work with clients).

Taking all this as a whole, how can you sum up your qualities as a counsellor?

Spend some time writing in response to these instructions:

1. Make a list of your gifts, glittering qualities and strengths as a counsellor;

2. Make a list of areas that might sometimes be personal limitations, gaps or 'blind spots' in your capacity to offer a counselling relationship;

3. Tell the story of at least one of the 'gifts' in a bit more detail: (i) what it was in your life that allowed you to develop this gift, and (ii) the effect this quality has on people you are helping;

4. Explore one of your limitations in a similar fashion: (i) what it was in your life that contributed to this limitation in your capacity to help, and (ii) the effect this limitation might have on people you are helping.

What are the implications, for you as a counsellor, of what you have written in response to these questions? What do your responses say about who you are, and what you stand for, as a counsellor?

Chapter 19 of *An Introduction to Counselling* offers a model for understanding counsellor development, in terms of seven dimensions of competence. How do the gifts and limitations you have identified fit into this model? Does the model suggest other gifts and limitations that you had not considered?

Looking ahead: when you reflect on what you have learned from this exercise, what are the implications for:

➡ The type of work you do as a counsellor (e.g. long-term or short-term, specific client groups and so on);

➡ Your future learning needs, for instance through training, supervision or personal study;

➡ Your role within the profession (as a supervisor, trainer, professional activist, writer, researcher).

Images of counselling

One of the key skills possessed by effective counsellors is sensitivity to language, to the ways in which people construct their emotional and interpersonal worlds through the words, images and metaphors that they use. An awareness of your own language use can also provide you with a creative means of exploring your own personal assumptions about counselling. In this activity, you are invited to find images and metaphors that capture the overall sense of what counselling means to you.

This task involves taking a few moments to reflect on the images and metaphors that come to mind when you think about different aspects of the counselling process.

Write whatever comes into your mind when you read the following questions:

? What kind of animal is a counsellor? A client?

? What kind of a sport is counselling?

? What kind of imagery comes to mind when you think about the process of counselling?

? The interaction between a counsellor and client is similar to...?

? A good counsellor or psychotherapist is like a...?

? Completing a series of counselling sessions is like...?

Many different types of images and metaphors may arise for you – write them all down. If possible, categorize these images and metaphors into themes. Look at each of the metaphors you have generated. Which aspects of counselling are *highlighted* by each metaphor, and which aspects are *downplayed*?

The significance of metaphors in counselling is also discussed on pages 342 and 474 of *An Introduction to Counselling.*

Once you have thought of the images and metaphors that strike a chord for you, you might wish to think about how they compare with the metaphors that underpin mainstream theories such as person-centred, psychodynamic and cognitive-behavioural. The idea that a root 'image of the person' underlies each of these theories is discussed in pages 231–3 of *An Introduction to Counselling.*

What have you learned from this task, about your own deeply-held attitudes and assumptions? What have you learned about your position in relation to mainstream theories?

The psychotherapy researcher Lisa Navajits asked a number of counsellors and therapists to write down their images for the therapy process. What she found is described on pages 287–8 of *An Introduction to Counselling.* Do her results include metaphors that surprise you, or which you disagree with? If so, what might this mean in relation to your personal approach as a counsellor?

Further reading

A fascinating book on the role of metaphor in human thought, which explains the highlighting/downplaying notion, is Lakoff, G. and Johnson, M. (1980) *Metaphors We Live by.* Chicago: University of Chicago Press.

What are you aiming to achieve as a counsellor? Selecting criteria for evaluating your effectiveness

One way of summing up your approach to counselling is to be able to be clear about what it is you believe that counselling is trying to achieve. What are the desired outcomes of counselling? There are many competing ideas about the appropriate criteria for assessing the effectiveness of counselling. Many research studies and counselling organizations use questionnaires that measure client change in terms of psychiatric categories such as depression and anxiety. Some practitioners view outcomes in terms of factors that are consistent with their theoretical approach. For example, person-centred counsellors look for change in self-esteem and self-acceptance, while cognitive-behaviour therapists seek change in observable behaviour and dysfunctional beliefs.

The CORE system is increasingly being used as an evaluation tool that provides an integrative focus, not rooted in any particular therapeutic model or ideology. The CORE questionnaire assesses client outcomes on four dimensions: subjective well-being, psychological symptoms, social and interpersonal functioning, and risk to self and others.

The *Just Therapy* centre in New Zealand, led by Charles Waldegrave, Kiwi Tamasese, Flora Tuhaka and Warihi Campbell, has developed an approach to therapy that draws on the traditions of the three main communities in their country: Maori, Samoan and Pakeha (European). They identify their criteria for effective work in the following way:

> …we have chosen three primary concepts that characterise our Just Therapy approach. When assessing the quality of our work, we measure it against the interrelationship of these three concepts. The first is belonging, which refers to the essence of identity, to who were are, our cultured and gendered histories, and our ancestry. The second is sacredness, which refers to the deepest respect for humanity, its qualities, and the environment. The third is liberation, which refers to freedom, wholeness and justice. We are interested in the inter-dependence of these concepts, not one without another. Not all stories of belonging are liberating, for example, and some experiences of liberation are not sacred. We are interested in the harmony between all three concepts as an expression of Just Therapy. (Waldegrave, 2003: 75)

Take a few moments to reflect on the outcome/effectiveness criteria that you use in your work as a counsellor. It may be helpful to think about clients who you might consider to be 'good outcome' cases, and some who you felt had 'poor outcomes'. What are the factors that made these cases seem 'good' or 'not so good'?

Make a list of the outcome criteria that are important for you.

What does this list say about who you are as a counsellor, and what you stand for?

Some widely-used outcome measures, including the CORE system, are described on pages 459–63 of *An Introduction to Counselling*.

The *Just Therapy* approach has been heavily influenced by narrative therapy, which is introduced on pages 234–40.

What's in your toolbox?

Counsellors can be divided into those who have toolboxes and those who do not. A toolbox is a personal store of ideas, exercises, stories and strategies that the counsellor can draw upon to facilitate the therapeutic process, or to move things on when the therapy seems to have reached an impasse.

An example of a counsellor's toolbox can be found in a brilliant book by Susan Carrell (2001), who describes more than 40 tools that she has acquired in over 20 years of practice. Some of these tools are tangible and take up space, for example a sand tray for adults. Others require only paper and pens, for instance a 'Life-Line' (timeline) exercise. Others are virtual tools, stored in the counsellor's head. For instance:

when your female client is agonizing over what to do about a difficult situation – her boyfriend is treating her poorly, a co-worker humiliated her, she suspects her husband is cheating her ... and she looks at you pleadingly seeking advice, ask her this question: What would you say to a girlfriend who came to you with this story? ... This question elicits responses that come from a deep place in a woman's psyche. It appeals to the sanctity of friendship between women and the long history of devotion that women friends have enjoyed ... Women know that boyfriends come and go, husbands come and go, children come and go, but girlfriends are forever. She will give her girlfriend (and thus, herself) the best advice ever. (p. 184)

Some therapists might argue that such tools are inevitably superficial and are no substitute, in the end, for the rigorous application of basic therapeutic principles, derived from a solid theory. But is this necessarily true? Maybe therapists who are grounded in a specific theory (unlike Susan Carrell, who could be perhaps be described as a pragmatic eclectic) merely carry a kit of tools that are selected on the basis of theoretical consistency (as well as effectiveness).

Irvin Yalom (2002) is a leading figure in existential psychotherapy – perhaps one of the least 'toolbox-oriented' therapies that could be imagined. Yet he has published what he has described as a 'nuts-and-bolts collection of favourite interventions' (p. xiv). These include guidelines for challenging clients ('strike while the iron is cold'), strategies for checking into the here-and-now each hour, suggestions for making home visits and interviewing the client's significant other, and much else.

> Debates over the relative merits of eclecticism versus theoretical purity are examined on pages 61–72 of An Introduction to Counselling.
>
> More on Yalom is on pages 273–7.

Instructions

Take a few minutes to list the items in your own therapeutic toolbox. Are there tools that you have once used, and have now discarded, or rarely employ? Are there tools that you would wish to include in your kitbox, or that you have acquired and are uncertain about using?

What do these tools signify about your identity as a counsellor?

Further reading

Mahoney, M.J. (2003) Constructive Psychotherapy: a Practical Guide. New York: Guilford Press.
Seiser, L. and Wastell, C. (2002) Interventions and Techniques. Buckingham: Open University Press.

Marketing yourself as a counsellor: the one-minute intro

Developing a coherent and integrated sense of who you are as a counsellor is not merely a personal development task. There are many situations where you may be called upon to explain or describe your approach, to different audiences. This exercise invites you to write your response to the following scenarios:

1. *The one-minute intro.* You are in a group situation where you have been given one minute to introduce yourself and your counselling approach. Perhaps you have been invited to discuss your work with some trainees on a counselling course, or you are being interviewed for a job as a counsellor, or you are joining a peer support group. What do you say about yourself?

2. *A leaflet.* You have been appointed as a counsellor in a health clinic, student counselling service, or some other setting. In order to help potential clients to access your service, you need to design a leaflet that describes your counselling approach and explains what is involved in being a client. What do you write?

3. *A website.* As a means of promoting your private practice work you decide to develop your own website. How do you describe yourself within this medium?

4. *An activity.* Imagine that you have been asked to facilitate a two-hour workshop with a group of students of nursing or social work, with the aim of helping them to learn about what your approach to counselling is about, at an experiential level. Is there one exercise or activity that might allow these students to go beyond a purely intellectual understanding of your approach?

After you have completed these tasks, you may find it interesting to carry out a survey of leaflets and websites composed by other practitioners. Reflect on the different ways in which other colleagues have approached the task of depicting their approach. What does the approach you have adopted say about who you are as a counsellor?

Further reading

Two writers who have explored their own struggle to characterize their approach, for external audiences, are:

Morgan, A. (1999) Practice notes: introducing narrative ways of working, in D. Denborough and C. White (eds) *Extending Narrative Therapy: a Collection of Narrative-based Papers.* Adelaide: Dulwich Centre Publications.

Sween, E. (1999) The one-minute question: what is narrative therapy?, in D. Denborough and C. White (eds) *Extending Narrative Therapy: a Collection of Narrative-based Papers.* Adelaide: Dulwich Centre Publications.

Your counselling room

The physical environment in which counselling takes place is an important, but seldom acknowledged, element of the counselling process. The furnishing and layout of a counselling room both raises expectations and sets limits regarding the ways in which a client can express himself or herself, how safe he or she feels, the extent to which movement is possible, and much else. The location of the room – the building, how accessible it is, what the waiting area is like – also sets the scene for the type of therapeutic work that can occur.

> The significance of the space within which counselling takes place is explored further on page 306 of *An Introduction to Counselling*.

Imagine your own *ideal* counselling room. In designing your therapeutic space, consider the following questions:

 What kind of building is the room in? Where is the building? What are the surroundings?

 How is the waiting area furnished and laid out? What does the client do while waiting?

 How is the counselling room furnished and laid out? What objects and images are in the room?

 What use is made of texture, colour, design, fragrance, sound and so on?

You may find it useful to make a sketch of this space.

Once you have constructed your image of an ideal counselling environment, reflect on these further questions:

 What are the main differences between your ideal therapy room and counselling spaces that you have visited or worked in? What does this comparison tell you about possible goals for the future?

 What have you learned about yourself and your personal approach as a counsellor, from this exercise? To what extent could your ideal therapy room be understood as a projection of your core values as a counsellor?

 In what ways does your design reflect the concepts and assumptions of your preferred theoretical approach(es)?

Building an effective support network

A critical aspect of developing a sense of professional identity as a counsellor involves finding ways of dealing with the stress and pressure that can result from this kind of work. The construction of survival strategies depends to a large extent on the existence of a support network, comprising colleagues, therapists, supervisors and other people who can contribute to the maintenance of work-life balance.

The purpose of this learning task is to invite reflection on the elements of your own personal, actual or intended support network, and to consider the ways in which this network reflects or expresses your identity as a counsellor.

Reflecting on your position in relation to supervision

⇒ Write a character sketch of your ideal supervisor;

⇒ Write a character sketch of what would be, for you, the 'supervisor from hell';

⇒ What do you need from supervision? What are you looking for?

⇒ What would it take (has it taken) to make you change your supervisor?

Reflecting on your position in relation to personal therapy

> Supervision is discussed on pages 507–14 of *An Introduction to Counselling.*
>
> The stress of being a counsellor is explored on pages 428–9 and 490–3.

⇒ Write a character sketch of your ideal therapist;

⇒ Write a character sketch of what would be, for you, the 'therapist from hell';

⇒ What do you need from your own therapy? What are you looking for?

⇒ What would it take (has it taken) to make you enter therapy?

Stress and coping

(?) What do you find most stressful in your work?

(?) What activities do you find most satisfying and nurturing in your work?

(?) What strategies do you employ to cope with stressful aspects of your work?

(?) What would it take to make you review these strategies?

Make some notes in response to these questions. Once you have done some writing, consider the following additional issues:

(?) How well are you supporting yourself?

(?) What impact does the kind of support network you have constructed have on your work with clients?

(?) What impact does the kind of support network you have constructed have on your life outside your work?

(?) What does your support network say about who you are, and what you stand for, as a counsellor?

Further reading

Dryden, W. (ed.) (1994) *The Stress of Counselling in Action*. London: Sage.

Horton, I. (ed.) (1997) *The Needs of Counsellors and Psychotherapists: Emotional, Social, Physical, Professional*. London: Sage.

Skovholt, T.M. (2001) *The Resilient Practitioner: Burnout Prevention and Self-care Strategies*. Boston: Allyn & Bacon.

Weaks, D. (2002) Unlocking the secrets of 'good supervision', *Counselling and Psychotherapy Research*, 2:33–9.

Your position in relation to research and inquiry

The primary focus of this Workbook has been to integrate the theory and practice of counselling within the narrative of your own personal life experience, with the goal of creating a 'knowledge base' that is firmly grounded in your everyday reality. However, it is important to acknowledge that there exists another knowledge base, which lies outside of personal experience – the knowledge that can be derived from systematic research.

In recent years, counselling and psychotherapy research has evolved in the direction of what is known as 'methodological pluralism'. In the past, research tended to mean statistics and experiments. Now, research and inquiry draw upon personal experience, interviews, action, stories, and much else. Current research therefore represents a potentially rich source of knowledge for practitioners.

What is your relationship with the knowledge base represented by systematic research and inquiry? Take some time to write your responses to the following questions:

> The main themes and methods in contemporary research in counselling are examined in Chapter 18 of *An Introduction to Counselling.*

(?) In principle, how important do you think research is in relation to counselling? What are the reasons for being interested in research at all?

(?) What are your criticisms of counselling research? What should or could researchers do in order to make research more relevant or useful?

(?) In what ways do you use research to inform your practice? List some research reports that you have recently read. How have these influenced how you think about your work as a counsellor?

(?) How do you access research? How often do you read about research findings?

(?) If you were in a position to have some free time to do research, which questions or topics would interest you?

Once you have responded to these questions, reflect on what you have discovered about who you are as a counsellor, and also about future directions that your career or interests might take.

What does it mean to be 'personal'?: some questions from Carl Rogers

In *On Becoming a Person*, Carl Rogers (1961) consistently returns to the theme that it is the person of the counsellor, and his or her capacity to enter into a non-judgemental relationship with the client, that makes a difference. Many passages in this book read like a conversation, with Rogers engaging in dialogue with aspects of his own experiencing, and attempting to open dialogue with his readers.

In Chapter 3, Rogers asks a series of questions that remain meaningful to anyone seeking to develop a personal approach to counselling:

1. Can I be in some way which will be perceived by the other person as trustworthy, dependable or consistent in some deep sense?

2. Can I be expressive enough as a person that what I am will be communicated unambiguously?

3. Can I let myself experience positive attitudes towards this other person – attitudes of warmth, caring, liking, interest, respect?

4. Can I be strong enough as a person to be separate from the other?

5. Am I secure enough within myself to permit his or her separateness? Can I permit him or her to be what he or she is?

6. Can I let myself enter fully into the world of his or her feelings and personal meanings and see these as he or she does?

7. Can I accept each facet of this other person when he or she presents it to me?

8. Can I act with sufficient sensitivity in the relationship that my behaviour will not be perceived as a threat?

9. Can I free the other from the threat of external evaluation?

10. Can I meet this other individual as a person who is in the process of becoming, or will I be bound by his past and by my past?

In the light of what you have written in response to other activities in this Workbook, and referring also to other relevant learning experiences, reflect on the following questions:

> These questions are placed in context in Chapter 6 of *An Introduction to Counselling*.

(?) Do Carl Rogers's questions capture, for you, an adequate sense of what it might mean to use a *personal* approach in your work as a counsellor? If not, which questions would you add, delete, or reword?

(?) Where are the areas of personal challenge for you, in relation to these aspects of a 'personal' approach?

Ten years from now

Imagine that the date is 10 years in the future. You have achieved all the main goals that you set yourself at the end of your period of counsellor training. You are in a peer support group, which has decided to devote a couple of sessions to giving each member time and space to review their career. You are being interviewed by these close colleagues, and invited to explore the following questions:

How do you sum up your work now – who you are in terms of your professional identity, where and how you work, and the approach you take?

In what ways is this current situation different from your working life 10 years ago?

What have been the main challenges and choice points for you during the last 10 years?

What have been your main sources of support and assistance, that have enabled you to achieve your aims?

What are the most important things you have learned over this period of time?

How have you changed, and how have you remained the same, as a person?

What would you like to say to the 'you' of 10 years ago?

Once you have responded to these questions, take some time to reflect on the implications of this piece of 'time travelling' for your professional identity now.

Core themes

On pages 518–22 of *An Introduction to Counselling*, the author describes five core themes that have been central for him. If at all possible, do not read these pages until you have identified your own core themes.

In your view, what is counselling about? What is it for? What are the core life themes and issues that people are faced with, and for which they use counselling as a way of resolving?

These questions define the heart of your personal approach as a counsellor.

Notes for tutors

This Workbook is intended as a resource to support those at the stage of basic training in counselling (in the UK, this would be Diploma level), rather than those participating in more introductory skills courses. As explained in the Introduction, the underlying philosophy of the Workbook is that counselling is an intensely personal activity, and that it is essential that theories and methods are assimilated and integrated into the counsellor's sense of who he or she is, rather than being ideas or techniques that are 'bolted on'.

At the heart of any training course is the capacity for the trainer to convey his or her 'truth' to the trainee, in the form of lectures, workshops and handouts that reflect the trainer's personal and professional experience. There is no way that this Workbook is intended to replace learning activities that a trainer or staff team have devised, or form the basis for a whole syllabus. The aim of the Workbook, instead, is to play a role as a supplement to an existing programme or curriculum.

There are a number of ways in which the Workbook might be used in the context of a counselling training programme:

Independent study/background reading. Many students on counselling courses are very keen to learn, and quickly work their way through recommended texts and reading lists. There is plenty in this Workbook to keep such students busy. Particularly if *An Introduction to Counselling* is the core text for the course, or one of a set of core texts, students are likely to find the Workbook valuable as a means of linking together themes and issues that are dealt with in different chapters, and making connections between concepts and personal experience.

Selecting specific learning tasks. Many counselling tutors and trainers like to organize classes on a workshop basis, with students engaging in an experiential exercise, or exploring case material, then coming back together for a group discussion. Many of the learning tasks in the Workbook may be applicable in such situations, and have the advantage of being referenced both to a textbook and to other activities that the student might wish to pursue. Because the learning tasks are presented in a workbook format, they can be given to students as 'homework' assignments, thus giving more time for participative work when the group actually gets together in class. The learning tasks and activities included in the Workbook encompass many of the central topics covered in most counselling courses: self-awareness, theory and ethical issues. The Workbook does not include inputs on counselling skills, or on preparation for practice, because these are topics that require direct tutor involvement and guidance.

As the basis for a peer or facilitator-led personal development group, learning set or study group. Although the Workbook is written in such a way as to make it possible for students to use it on an individual basis, the majority of the learning tasks are likely to produce deeper and more significant learning if they are shared in an on-going small group. The Introduction section of the Workbook includes some guidelines for learners who might wish to work on Workbook activities in a group setting.

The Workbook can be valuable in relation to student assessment. On some courses, students are required to submit a Personal Journal, or report based on their Personal

Journal. In this situation, it may be helpful to point students in the direction of relevant Workbook activities, for example in the opening section, as a focus for at least some of the content of their Personal Journal. The Workbook also includes a page on keeping a Learning Journal. Another assessment possibility is to base assignments on specific learning tasks. Almost all of the tasks involve doing some writing. By indicating a limit to this writing (e.g. 1000–1500 words), and maybe also requiring the student to discuss their self-exploration in the context of relevant theory and research (material in *An Introduction to Counselling* can serve as the staring point for such discussion), almost all of the learning tasks/activities could form the basis for coursework assignments. A third possibility, in relation to assessment, is to invite students to submit a portfolio of their writing, done in response to learning tasks, along with a concluding section which reflects on and integrates their learning. This assignment format is an excellent way to encourage student initiative and creativity, since they will all choose different combinations of learning tasks, and all of their answers are, inevitably, original (there is nowhere that they could find the answer to a learning task already written in a book or article – the only answer is their personal one). One highly challenging variant on the portfolio assessment option is to ask students to integrate their pieces of writing into a statement of their *personal philosophy of counselling*. However, some students will find this a very hard thing to do. Being on a journey towards a sense of professional identity, or a personal approach, is one thing – being able to articulate it is something else.

Internet resources and further reading

One of the recurring themes that weaves through this Workbook is the idea that becoming a counsellor is like being on a journey. This is a lengthy journey – to develop a sense of competence, and a secure professional identity as a counsellor can take between 3 and 5 years. The most important type of assistance that anyone can have on a journey is other people, such as guides and mentors, fellow travellers. But there are other resources that can be helpful too. In this section, some suggestions for potentially useful 'tools for a counsellors' journey' are assembled.

Internet resources

There is an ever-increasing range of websites that carry information about theory, research and practice in counselling and psychotherapy. An up-to-date set of links can be found through the website for this book: www.openup.co.uk/mcleod.

Therapy thrillers

It is worthwhile asking experienced counsellors and psychotherapists about special books that have inspired them. Sometimes they will mention serious theoretical books. Very occasionally they may refer to books that are research-based. But most often, they will point you in the direction of 'therapy thrillers' – gripping stories that are drawn from personal experience. Two of the most popular books in this category are:

Axline, V. (1971) *Dibs: In Search of Self*. London: Penguin. A case study of play therapy with a young boy – captures the spirit of the client-centred approach.

Peck, M.S. (1978) *The Road Less Traveled: A New Psychology of Love, Traditional Values and Spiritual Growth*. New York: Simon & Schuster. A book which many therapists have found highly meaningful, as a source of inspiration regarding the possibility of growth and change.

The experiences of people undergoing therapy training

There are always stages in a long journey that are demanding, exhausting or hazardous. At these times it can be useful to know that other people have travelled the same road, and survived. There are several excellent books that have brought together trainees' accounts of aspects of the experience of becoming a counsellor:

Alred, G., Davies, G., Hunt, K. and Davies, V.H. (eds) (2004) *Experiences of Counsellor Training: Challenge, Surprise and Change*. London: Palgrave.

Buchanan, L. and Hughes, R. (2001) *Experiences of Person-centred Training: A Compendium of Case Studies to Assist Prospective Applicants*. Ross-on-Wye: PCCS Books.

Dryden, W. and Spurling, L. (eds) (1989) *On Becoming a Psychotherapist*. London: Tavistock/Routledge.

Dryden, W. and Thorne, B. (eds) (1991) *Training and Supervision for Counselling in Action*. London: Sage.

Johns, H. (ed.) (1998) *Balancing Acts: Studies in Counselling Training*. London: Routledge.

Noonan, E. and Spurling, L. (eds) (1992) *The Making of a Counsellor*. London: Routledge.

White, C. and Hales, J. (eds) (1997) *The Personal is the Professional: Therapists Reflect on their Families, Lives and Work*. Adelaide: Dulwich Centre Publications.

Applied wisdom: learning from those who have been there

A particularly interesting area of research, pioneered by Thomas Skovholt and Helge Ronnestad (1995), has examined the experiences and characteristics of therapists who have been successful within the profession, in the sense of being recognized by their colleagues as 'the best of the best', or who have worked as therapists for a long time, and are able to look back on a rich and varied career. These studies have been written up in an accessible and stimulating manner, and have a lot to offer to anyone seeking to know more about the realities of a career as a therapist.

Ronnestad, M.H. and Skovholt, T.M. (2001) Learning arena for professional development: retrospective accounts of senior psychotherapists, *Professional Psychology: Research and Practice*, 32:181–7. Analysis of interviews with some very experienced therapists.

Skovholt, T.M. (2001) *The Resilient Practitioner: Burnout Prevention and Self-care Strategies*. Boston: Allyn & Bacon. Considers the implications of research in terms of strategies for surviving the stress of being a counsellor.

Skovholt, T.M. and Jennings, L. (eds) (2004) *Master Therapists: Exploring Expertise in Therapy and Counseling*. Boston: Allyn & Bacon. Examines the attitudes and competencies of therapists considered to be the leaders of the profession.

Personal development guidebooks

There are other books that, like this Workbook, provide reading material and learning activities that are designed to encourage the development of a personally-grounded approach to counselling. Particularly recommended are:

Corey, M.S. and Corey, G. (2003) *Becoming a Helper*. Pacific Grove, CA: Brooks/Cole.

Cross, M.C. and Papadopoulos, L. (2001) *Becoming a Therapist: A Manual for Personal and Professional Development*. Hove: Brunner-Routledge.

References

Adams, K. (1990) *Journal to the Self*. New York: Warner Books.

Alred, G., Favies, G., Hunt, K. and Davies, V.H. (eds) (2004) *Experiences of Counsellor Training: Challenge, Surprise and Change*. London: Palgrave.

Angus, L.E. and McLeod, J. (eds) (2004) *Handbook of Narrative and Psychotherapy: Practice, Theory and Research*. Thousand Oaks, CA: Sage.

Atwood, G. and Stolorow, R. (1993) *Faces in a Cloud: Intersubjectivity in Personality Theory*. Northvale, NJ: Jason Aronson.

Axline, V. (1971) *Dibs: In Search of Self*. London: Penguin.

Bachelor, A. (1988) How clients perceive therapist empathy: a content analysis of 'received' empathy, *Psychotherapy*, 25:227–40.

Berne, E. (1975) *What Do You Say After You Say Hello? The Psychology of Human Destiny*. London: Corgi.

Bettelheim, B. (1976) *The Uses of Enchantment: The Meaning and Importance of Fairy Tales*. London: Penguin.

Bolton, G., Howlett, S., Lago, C. and Wright, J.K. (eds) (2004) *Writing Cures: An Introductory Handbook of Writing in Counselling and Psychotherapy*. London: Brunner-Routledge.

Book, H. (2004) The CCRT approach to working with patient narratives in psychodynamic psychotherapy, in L. Angus and J. McLeod (eds) *Handbook of Narrative and Psychotherapy: Practice, Theory and Research*. Thousand Oaks, CA: Sage.

Bruch, M. and Bond, F.W. (1998) *Beyond Diagnosis: Case Formulation Approach in CBT*. Chichester: Wiley

Buchanan, L. and Hughes, R. (2001) *Experiences of Person-centred Training: A Compendium of Case Studies to Assist Prospective Applicants*. Ross-on-Wye: PCCS Books.

Burns, G.A. (1998) *Nature-Guided Therapy: Brief Interventiion Strategies for Health and Well-Being*. London: Taylor and Francis.

Carrell, S. (2001) *The Therapist's Toolbox: 26 Tools and an Assortment of Implements for the Busy Therapist*. Thousand Oaks, CA: Sage.

Clark, A. (2002) *Early Recollections: Theory and Practice in Counseling and Psychotherapy*. New York: Brunner-Routledge.

Clarkson, P. (1994) The psychotherapeutic relationship, in P. Clarkson and M. Pokorny (eds) *The Handbook of Psychotherapy*. London: Routledge.

Cohen, D. (1997) *Carl Rogers. A Critical Biography*. London: Constable.

Cohen, L. (1994) Phenomenology of theraputic reading, with implications for research and practice of bibliotherapy, *The Arts in Psychotherapy*, 21:37–44.

Combs, A. (1986) What makes a good helper? A Person-Centred approach, *Person-Centred Review*, 1:51–61.

Combs, A. (1990) *A Theory of Therapy*. London: Sage.

Corey, M.S. and Corey, G. (2003) *Becoming a Helper*. Pacific Grove, CA: Brooks/Cole.

Cross, M.C. and Papadopoulos, L. (2001) *Becoming a Therapist: A Manual for Personal and Professional Development*. Hove: Brunner-Routledge.

Csikzentmihalyi, M. and Beattie, O. (1979) Life themes: a theoretical and empirical exploration of their origins and effects, *Journal of Humanistic Psychology*, 19:45–63.

Davies, D. and Neal, C. (eds) (1996) *Pink Therapy: A Guide for Counsellors and Therapists Working with Gay, Lesbian and Bisexual Clients*. Buckingham: Open University Press.

Dryden, W. (ed.) (1986) *Key Cases in Psychotherapy*. London: Croom Helm.

Dryden, W. (ed.) (1994) *The Stress of Counselling in Action*. London: Sage.

Dryden, W. and Spurling, L. (eds) (1989) *On Becoming a Psychotherapist*. London: Tavistock/Routledge.

Dryden, W. and Thorne, B. (eds) (1991) *Training and Supervision for Counselling in Action*. London: Sage.

Dyche, L. and Zayas, L.H. (1995) The value of curiosity and naivete for the cross-cultural psychotherapist, *Family Process*, 34:389–99.

Edwards, D. and Jacobs, M. (2003) *Conscious and Unconscious*. Buckingham: Open University Press.

Eells, T.D. (ed.) (1997) *Handbook of Psychotherapy Case Formulation*. New York: Guilford Press.

Farber, B.A., Brink, D.C. and Raskin, P.M. (eds) (1996) *The Psychotherapy of Carl Rogers: Cases and Commentary*. New York: Guilford Press.

Fear, R. and Woolfe, R. (1996) Searching for integration in counselling practice, *British Journal of Guidance and Counselling*, 24:399–412.

Fowler, J.C., Hilsenroth, M.J. and Handler, L. (2000) Martin Mayman's early memories technique: Bridging the gap between personality assessment and psychotherapy, *Journal of Personality Assessment*, 75:18–32.

Freud, S. (1933) *New Introductory Lectures on Psychoanalysis*. London: Hogarth Press.

Freud, S. (1938) *An Outline of Psychoanalysis*. London: Hogarth Press.

Fuhriman, A., Barlow, S. and Wanlass, J. (1989) Words, imagination, meaning: towards change, *Psychotherapy*, 26:149–60.

Gay, P. (1988) *Freud: A Life for our Time*. London: Dent.

Gay. P. (1995) *The Freud Reader*. London: Vintage.

Gendlin, E. (1967) Subverbal communication and therapist expressivity: trends in client-centered therapy with schizophrenics, in C. Rogess and B. Stevens (eds) *Person to Person: The Problem of Being Human*. San Francisco: Real People Press.

Goss, S. and Anthony, K. (eds) (2003) *Technology in Counselling and Psychotherapy: A Practitioner's Guide*. London: Palgrave Macmillan.

Haley, J. (1969) The art of being a failure as a psychotherapist, *American Journal of Orthopsychiatry*, 39:691–5.

Honey, P. and Mumford, A. (2000) *The Learning Styles Questionnaire*. Maidenhead: Peter Honey Learning.

Horton, I. (ed.) (1997) *The Needs of Counsellors and Psychotherapists: Emotional, Social, Physical, Professional*. London: Sage.

House, R. and Totton, N. (eds) (1998) *Implausible Professions: Arguments for Pluralism and Autonomy in Psychotherapy and Counselling*. Ross-on-Wye: PCCS Books.

Howard, A. (2000) *Philosophy for Counselling and Psychotherapy: Pythagoras to Post-modernism*. London: Macmillan.

Hunter, M. and Struve, J. (1998) *The Ethical Use of Touch in Psychotherapy*. Thousand Oaks, CA: Sage.

James, R. and Gilliland, B. (2001) *Crisis Intervention Strategies*. Belmont, CA: Wadsworth.

Johns, H. (ed.) (1998) *Balancing Acts: Studies in Counselling Training*. London: Routledge.

Josselson, R. (1996) *The Space Between Us: Exploring the Dimensions of Human Relation-ships*. Thousand Oaks, CA: Sage.

Kanel, K. (1999) *A Guide to Crisis Intervention*. Belmont, CA: Wadsworth.

Kirschenbaum, H. (1979) *On Becoming Carl Rogers*. New York: Dell.

Kolb, D.A. (1984) *Experiential Learning: Experience as the Source of Learning and Development*. Englewood Cliffs, NJ: Prentice-Hall.

Kvale, S. (1992) Postmodern psychology: a contradiction in terms?, in S. Kvale (ed.) *Psychology and Postmodernism*. London: Sage.

Lakoff, G. and Johnson, M. (1980) *Metaphors We Live By*. Chicago: University of Chicago Press.

Lange, A., Schoutrop, M., Schrieken, B. and Ven, J-P. (2002) Interapy: a model for therapeutic writing through the internet, in S.J. Lepore and J.M. Smyth (eds) *The Writing Cure; How Expressive Writing Promotes Health and Emotional Well-being*. Washington: American Psychological Association.

Lewchanin, S. and Zubrod, L.A. (2001) Choices in life: a clinical tool for facilitating midlife review, *Journal of Adult Development*, 8:193–6.

Lietaer, G. (1993) Authenticity, congruence and transparency, in D. Brazier (ed.) *Beyond Carl Rogers*. London: Constable.

Loewenthal, D. and Snell, R. (2003) *Post-modernism for Psychotherapists: A Critical Reader*. London: Brunner-Routledge.

Lomas, P. (1981) *The Case for a Personal Psychotherapy*. Oxford: Oxford University Press.

Lomas, P. (1999) Interview with Peter Lomas (Sian Morgan), in L. King (ed.) *Committed Uncertainty: Essays in Honour of Peter Lomas*. London: Whurr.

Loo, C.M. (1974) The self-puzzle. A diagnostic and therapeutic tool, *Journal of Personality*, 42:236–42.

Lott, D.A. (1999) *In Session: The Bond between Women and their Therapists*. New York: W.H. Freeman.

Luborsky, L. and Crits-Christoph, P. (eds) (1990) *Understanding Transference: The CCRT Method*. New York: Basic Books.

McAdams, D.P. (1993) *The Stories We Live By: Personal Myths and the Making of the Self*. New York: William Murrow.

McAdams, D. (2000) *The Person: An Integrated Introduction*. New York: Wiley.

McAdams, D.P., Hoffman, B.J., Mansfield, E.D. and Day, R. (1996) Themes of agency and communion in significant autobiographical scenes, *Journal of Personality*, 64:339–77.

McConnaughy, E.A. (1987) The person of the therapist in therapeutic practice, *Psychotherapy*, 24:303–14.

McGoldrick, M. (ed.) (1998) *Re-visioning Family Therapy: Race, Culture and Gender in Clinical Practice*. New York: Guilford Press.

McLeod, J. (1997) *Narrative and Psychotherapy*. London: Sage.

McLeod, J. (2003) *An Introduction to Counselling*. Buckingham: Open University Press.

MacIntyre, A. (1981) *After Virtue: A Study in Moral Theory*. London: Duckworth.

Mahoney, M.J. (2003) *Constructive Psychotherapy: A Practical Guide*. New York: Guilford Press.

Marrow, A.J. (1977) *The Practical Theorist: The Life and Work of Kurt Lewin*. New York: Teachers' Press.

Mayman, M. (1968) Early memories and character structure, *Journal of Projective Techniques & Personality Assessment*, 32:303–16.

Mayman, M. and Faris, M. (1960) Early memories as expressions of relationship paradigms, *American Journal of Orthopsychiatry*, 30:507–20.

Mearns, D. and Thorne, B. (1999) *Person-centred Counselling in Action*. London: Sage.

Mearns, D. and Thorne, B. (2000) *Person-centred Therapy Today: New Frontiers in Theory and Practice*. London: Sage.

Monte, C. (1998) *Beneath the Mask: An Introduction to Theories of Personality*. New York: Wiley.

Moodley, R., Lago, C. and Talahite, C. (2004) *Carl Rogers Counsels a Black Client: Race and Culture in Person-centred Counselling*. Ross-on-Wye: PCCS Books.

Morgan, A. (1999) Practice notes: introducing narrative ways of working, in D. Denborough and C. White (eds) *Extending Narrative Therapy: A Collection of Narrative-based Papers*. Adelaide: Dulwich Centre Publications.

Morgan, A. (2000) *What is Narrative Therapy? An Easy-to-read Introduction*. Adelaide: Dulwich Centre Publications.

Noonan, E. and Spurling, L. (eds) (1992) *The Making of a Counsellor*. London: Routledge.

Peck, M.S. (1978) *The Road Less Traveled: A New Psychology of Love, Traditional Values and Spiritual Growth*. New York: Simon & Schuster.

Pennebaker, J. (1997) *Opening Up: The Healing Power of Expressing Emotions*. New York: Guilford Press.

Pervin, L. (2000) *Personality: Theory and Research*. New York: Wiley.

Pervin, L. (2002) *Current Controversies and Issues in Personality*. New York: Wiley.

Polkinghorne, D.E. (1992) Postmodern epistemology of practice, in S. Kvale (ed.) *Psychology and Postmodernism*. London: Sage.

Rainer, T. (1978) *The New Diary*. London: Angus and Robertson.

Rainer, T. (1997) *Your Life as Story: Writing the New Autobiography*. New York: G.P. Putnam.

Rogers, C.R. (1961) *On Becoming a Person*. London: Constable.

Rogers, C.R. (1975) Empathic: an unappreciated way of being, *Counseling Psychologist*, 5: 2–10.

Rogers, Carl (1980) *A Way of Being*. Boston, MA: Houghton Mifflin.

Romme, M. and Escher, S. (1993) *Making Sense of Voices*. London: Mind.

Ronnestad, M.H. and Skovholt, T.M. (2001) Learning arena for professional development: retrospective accounts of senior psychotherapists, *Professional Psychology: Research and Practice*, 32:181–7.

Rowan, J. (1993) *The Transpersonal, Counselling and Psychotherapy*. London: Routledge.

Rowan, J. and Jacobs, M. (2002) *The Therapist's Use of Self*. Buckingham: Open University Press.

Rutter, P. (1989) *Sex in the Forbidden Zone*. London: Mandala.

Seiser, L. and Wastell, C. (2002) *Interventions and Techniques*. Buckingham: Open University Press.

Shepard, M. (1975) *Fritz*. New York: Bantam Books.

Shlien, J. (1984) A counter-theory of transference, in R.F. Levant and J.M. Shlien (eds) *Client-centered Therapy and the Person-Centered Approach: New Directions in Theory, Research and Practice*. New York: Praeger.

Skovholt, T.M. (2001) *The Resilient Practitioner: Burnout Prevention and Self-care Strategies*. Boston: Allyn & Bacon.

Skovholt, T.M. and Jennings, L. (eds) (2004) *Master Therapists: Exploring Expertise in Therapy and Counseling*. Boston: Allyn & Bacon.

Skovholt, T.M. and Ronnestad, M.H. (1995) *The Evolving Professional Self: Themes in Counselor and Therapist Development*. New York: Wiley.

Strupp, H. (1978) The therapist's theoretical orientation: an overrated variable, *Psychotherapy*, 15:314–17.

Sween, E. (1999) The one-minute question: what is narrative therapy?, in D. Denborough and C. White (eds) *Extending Narrative Therapy: A Collection of Narrative-based Papers*. Adelaide: Dulwich Centre Publications.

Thompson, K. (2004) Journal writing as a therapeutic tool, in G. Bolton, S. Howlett, C. Lago and J. Wright (eds) *Writing Cures: An Introductory Handbook of Writing in Counselling and Psychotherapy*. London: Brunner-Routledge.

Thorne, B. and Dryden, W. (eds) (1993) *Counselling: Interdisciplinary Perspectives*. Buckingham: Open University Press.

Tjeltveit, A. (1998) *Ethics and Values in Psychotherapy*. London: Routledge.

Tune, D. (2001) Is touch a valid therapeutic intervention? Early returns from a qualitative study of therapists' views, *Counselling and Psychotherapy Research*, 1:167–71.

Waldegrave, C. (2003) 'Just Therapy' with families and communities, in C. Waldegrave, K. Tamasese, F. Tuhaka and W. Campbell (eds) *Just Therapy – A Journey*. Adelaide: Dulwich Centre Publications.

Weaks, D. (2002) Unlocking the secrets of 'good supervision', *Counselling and Psychotherapy Research*, 2:33–9.

Wedding, D. and Corsini, R.J. (eds) (2000) *Case Studies in Psychotherapy*. Itasca, IL: FE Peacock.

West, W. (2000) *Psychotherapy and Spirituality*. London: Sage

White, M. (1997) *Narratives of Therapists' Lives*. Adelaide: Dulwich Centre Publications.

White, C. and Hales, J. (eds) (1997) *The Personal is the Professional: Therapists Reflect on their Families, Lives and Work*. Adelaide: Dulwich Centre Publications.

Wosket, V. (1999) *The Therapeutic Use of Self: Counselling Practice, Research and Supervision*. London: Routledge.

Yalom, I. (1989) *Love's Executioner*. London: Penguin.

Yalom, I. (2002) *The Gift of Therapy: Reflections on Being a therapist*. London: Piatkus.

Index

AN INTRODUCTION TO COUNSELLING

Third Edition

John McLeod

Reviews of the second edition:

It is impossible to do justice to such an exhaustive, broad-based and very readable work in a short review. Professor McLeod has been meticulous, and with true scientific impartiality has looked at, studied and described the many strands and different schools of thought and methods that can lead towards successful counselling.

Therapy Weekly

This is a fascinating, informative, comprehensive and very readable book ... McLeod has produced a text that offers a great deal no matter what your level of competence or knowledge.

Journal of Interprofessional Care

One of the book's strengths is McLeod's willingness to go beyond a history of the development of counselling or a beginner's technical manual ... [and to] consider the political dimensions of counselling and the relevance of power to counselling relationships. A worthwhile acquisition for therapeutic community members, whatever their discipline or background.

Therapeutic Communities

This thoroughly revised and expanded version of the best-selling text *An Introduction to Counselling* provides a comprehensive introduction to the theory and practice of counselling and therapy. It is written in a clear, accessible style, covers all the core approaches to counselling, and takes a critical, questioning approach to issues of professional practice. Placing each counselling approach in its social and historical context, the book also introduces a wide range of contemporary approaches, including narrative therapy, systemic, feminist and multicultural.

This third edition includes a new chapter on the important emerging approach of philosophical counselling, and a chapter on the counselling relationship, as well as expanded coverage of attachment theory, counselling on the Internet, and solution-focused therapy. The text has been updated throughout, with additional illustrative vignettes and case studies.

Current comprehensive and readable, *An Introduction to Counselling* is a classic introduction to its subject.

640pp   0 335 21189 5 (Paperback)   0 335 21190 9 (Hardback)

ON TRAINING TO BE A THERAPIST

The Long and Winding Road to Qualification

John Karter

Having become aware during his own training of the enormous and varied pressures that students of psychotherapy and counselling have to face, often without any real source of support, the author seeks to explore the professional and personal difficulties, anxieties, emotions and pitfalls engendered by this unique and often destabilizing process from what he terms a 'student's eye view'.

Trainees frequently feel overwhelmed by an exhausting round of studying, clinical placements, supervision and personal therapy, and are often engaged in a juggling act between training, family and work. The fundamental objective of the book is to confront and to ameliorate these demands and difficulties and to highlight the fact that therapy training can and should be an enjoyable and fulfilling process in itself.

Among the many issues looked at are the ways in which training can change us as people, how it can affect our personal relationships, the dangers of adhering too strictly to theory, the terrors of essay writing, difficult issues with clients such as unplanned contact and sexuality, making the most of supervision, personal therapy, and many more.

On Training to be a Therapist has been designed for use as a standard text on training courses at all levels. It is aimed principally at psychotherapy and counselling students, but will also appeal to qualified practitioners, tutors and supervisors looking for a different perspective.

Contents
Foreword by Michael Jacobs – Introduction – Facing up to mission impossible – A change for the better? – The art of survival on the long and winding road – The dangers in playing it by the book – Super-vision syndrome and how to avoid it – Caution: slow go area ahead – Up close and personal – The bitter-sweet taste of freedom – Bibliography – Index.

176pp   0 335 21001 5 (Paperback)   0 335 21002 3 (Hardback)